Give Me Five!

ACTIVITY BOOK 2

My name is _____.

Joanne Ramsden • Donna Shaw

Course consultants: Rocío Gutiérrez Burgos and Mónica Pérez Is

macmillan education

CW01475722

Starter Unit Let's go back to school!

1 Circle the odd one out. Write and say.

1
apple   pear   banana   pencil

_____pencil_____

2
square   circle   cat   rectangle

_____

3
flower   dog   sheep   cow

_____

4
orange   pencil   rubber   ruler

_____

5
seven   six   oval   nine

_____

2 Look, read and write.

1 What's his name?

His ____name is____ Jake.

2 What's __her__ name?

_____.

3 What's _____?

_____.

4 What's _____?

_____.

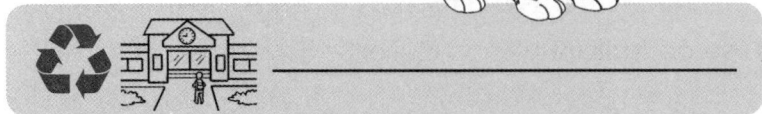

1 Follow and colour.

1 Arts and Crafts

2 Science

3 Music

4 Maths

5 ICT

6 PE

7 English

8 Spanish

$4+2 = 6$
$8-5 = 3$

¡Hola!

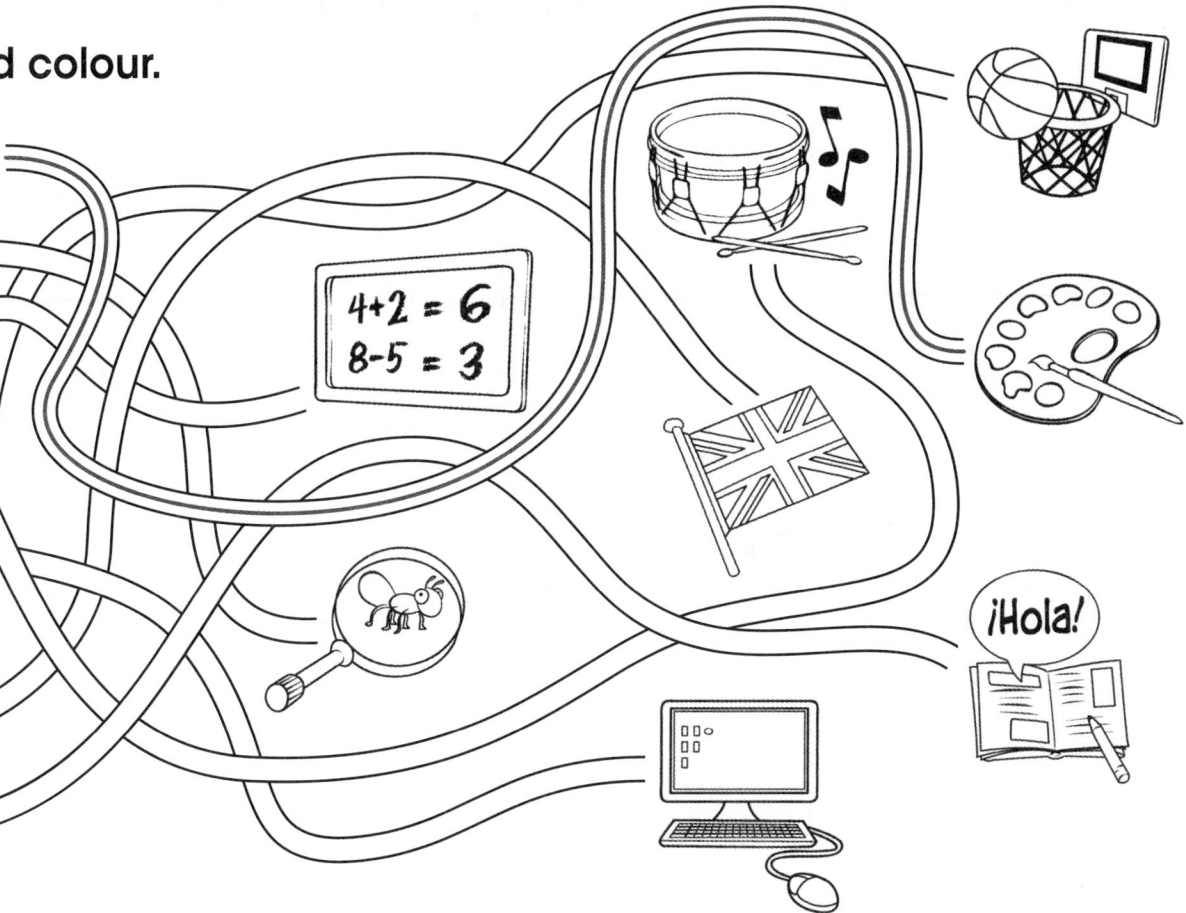

2 Ask your classmates. Write.

What's your favourite subject?

My favourite subject is _____. What's yours?

Name	Favourite subject

_____

1 Help Toby find his bone. Listen and colour the words. Write.

CD1 10

C	D	E	F
B	G	J	Z
A	T	H	S
M	I	L	K

S	Z	J	L
P	A	O	H
X	N	I	S
D	B	M	P

A	L	I	S
A	G	Y	H
E	N	F	M
B	C	O	P

1 _____Maths_____ 2 _____ 3 _____

S	C	I	A
T	F	E	N
P	B	R	C
V	D	X	E

M	U	O	L
Z	S	I	C
B	F	P	A
R	N	B	D

S	C	M	A
R	H	O	X
S	Z	O	L
T	B	Y	W

4 _____ 5 _____ 6 _____

2 **Talk Partners** Write and say the alphabet. Play the game.

7 k g b a 6 t z

C-A-T cat!

After you read

1 Remember the story. Number and write.

cloudy

sunny

raining

stormy

It's _____ today.

It's _____.

It's _____ again.

It's very __*sunny*__ today.

2 What's the weather like today? Write and draw.

It's _____.

3 **My progress** Make your traffic light. Listen to the teacher and point.

Teacher's Resource Bank

Key for Activity 3: **1.** I can say the school subjects. **2.** I can name different types of weather. **3.** I can ask and answer about my friend's name. **4.** I can ask and answer about my favourite subject. **5.** I listen to the teacher. **6.** I listen to other pupils.

Unit 1 **Move your body**

1 **Read and match. Say.**

1 I play volleyball and football.

2 I go cycling and swimming.

3 I play basketball and hockey.

4 I go skateboarding and rollerblading.

5 I play tennis and baseball.

2 **Look and write. Tick (✓) and say the sports you do.**

basketball   football   ~~tennis~~   swimming   cycling   skateboarding

I play ___tennis___ .

I go _____ .

I play _____ .

I go _____ .

I play _____ .

I go _____ .

_____

1 **Read and write. Follow and circle.**

play   go

1 Do you ___play___ volleyball?

2 Do you _____ cycling?

3 Do you _____ basketball?

4 _____ swimming?

5 _____ hockey?

Yes, I do.
No, I don't.

Yes, I do.
No, I don't.

Yes, I do.
No, I don't.

Yes, I do.
No, I don't.

Yes, I do.
No, I don't.

2 **Talk Partners** **Write a conversation. Act out.**

Do you _____?

_____. And I _____.

Do you _____, too?

_____.

Do you play tennis?

Yes, I do. And I go swimming.

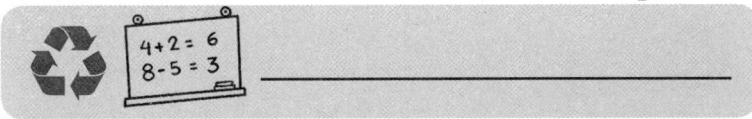

4 + 2 = 6
8 - 5 = 3   _____

After you read

1 Remember the story. Write and match.

rollerblading   baseball   ~~swimming~~   basketball   football   tennis

1 I go _____ swimming _____   on Monday.

2 I play _____   on Tuesday.

3 I play _____   on Wednesday.

4 I go _____   on Thursday.

5 I play _____   on Friday.

6 I play _____   on Saturday.

2 What sports do you play? Write and draw.

I play _____
on _____ .

I go _____
on _____ .

1 Listen and circle the actions. CD1 21

1
a b c d e

2
a b c d e

3
a b c d e

2 Look and write.

~~jumps~~   catches   hits   throws   bounces   kicks

Remember

he   she

1 She _____jumps_____.

2 He _____ the ball.

3 She _____ the ball.

4 _____ the ball.

5 _____
_____.

6 _____
_____.

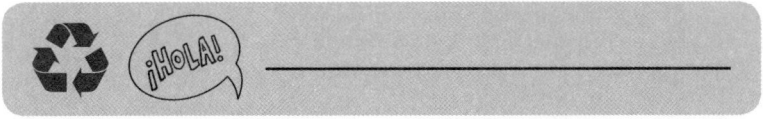

¡HOLA! _____

Toby's tongue twister

1 Write and say.

ai – ay. Sn _ai_ ls pl____ in the r ____n all d____.

2 Colour the 'ai' words red and the 'ay' words blue. Say.

rain	day	May	Spain	play
snail	train	say	rainbow	Tuesday

3 **Talk Partners** Play *Snap* in pairs.

1, 2, 3 snail!

1, 2, 3 play!

Snap!

1, 2, 3 say!

1, 2, 3 say!

Snap!

Play *Snap*: Pupils play with their Talk Partner. Pupils individually think of a word, count to three together, point to the picture and say the word. If the words are the same, they say *Snap!* If they are different, they continue playing the game.

1 **Listen and number. Write.** CD1 25

~~sack race~~   egg and spoon race   balloon toss   wheelbarrow race

_____   _____   sack race   _____

_____   _____   _____   _____

Think about your culture

What sports do you play at school?

2 **Read and tick (✓). Draw, write and say.**

1 I do the sack race.   ◯

2 I play basketball.   ◯

3 I throw and catch a balloon.   ◯

4 I do the wheelbarrow race.   ◯

5 I run and jump.   ◯

I _____.

_____

After you read

Text type: **A poem**

1 Remember the poem. Number.

Underarm,
Overarm.
BALL!

◯

Football,
Basketball,
Volleyball,
Any ball!

◯

Big ball,
Small ball,
Tennis ball,
Hockey ball.

①

Catch me!
Bounce me!
Kick me!
Throw me!

◯

2 Choose and write your own poem. Act out.

Small
Tennis Hockey
Big
Football
Volleyball
Basketball

_____ ball,

_____ ball,

_____ ball,

_____ ball.

_____ ,

_____ ,

_____ ,

Any ball!

_____ me!

_____ me!

_____ me!

_____ me!

Underarm,

Overarm.

BALL!

Hit   Kick
Catch   Throw
Bounce

_____

Remember
he / she kick**s**
he / she catch**es**

1 **Look and write.**

1. He _____jumps_____.

2. She _____ the ball.

3. _____ the ball.

4. _____ the ball.

5. _____ the ball.

6. _____.

2 **Talk Partners** Look and write. Ask and answer.

1. Do you play ____hockey____?

2. Do you go _____?

3. _____?

4. _____?

3 **My progress** Use your traffic light. Listen to the teacher and point.

Key for Activity 3: **1.** I can say the names of sports.
2. I can ask and answer about different sports and
actions. **3.** I can read a poem. **4.** I can write a poem.
5. I listen to the teacher and my friends.

_____

Joining in

1 What sports do they join in with? Listen and tick (✓). CD1 30

1

 ✓

3

2

4

21 CHANNEL

What sports do you join in with?

2 Read and tick (✓). Draw, point and say.

1 I do the egg and spoon race.

2 I do the tug of war.

3 I do the sack race.

4 I do the three-legged race.

I join in with the _____.

♻ **3** _____

Let's practise spelling!

Look	Copy	Cover and write
1 hockey	_____	_____
2 baseball	_____	_____
3 tennis	_____	_____
4 football	_____	_____
5 swimming	_____	_____
6 rollerblading	_____	_____
7 cycling	_____	_____
8 basketball	_____	_____
9 volleyball	_____	_____
10 skateboarding	_____	_____

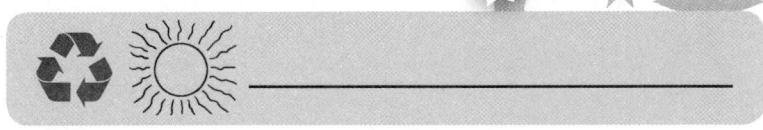

♻️ ☀️ _____

Let's go shopping!

1 **Read and match.**

1 bread and pineapple

2 tomatoes and potatoes

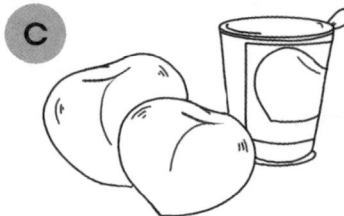

3 sweets and lemons

4 yoghurt and peaches

5 green beans and carrots

2 **What's in the bag? Draw and write.**

sweets   lemons   ~~bread~~   potatoes   green beans
carrots   tomatoes   yoghurt   pineapple   peaches

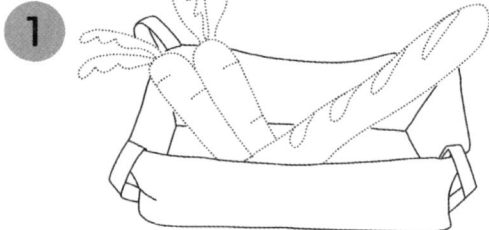

1

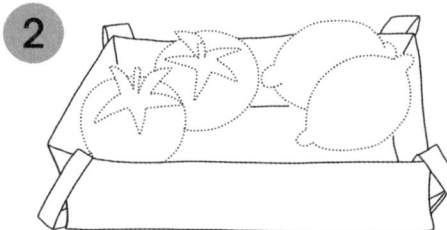

2

___bread___ and _____

_____ and _____

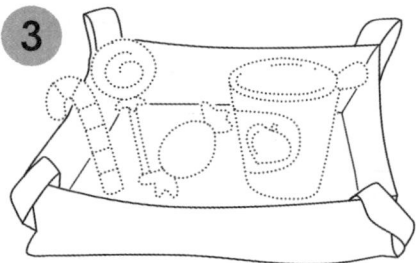

3

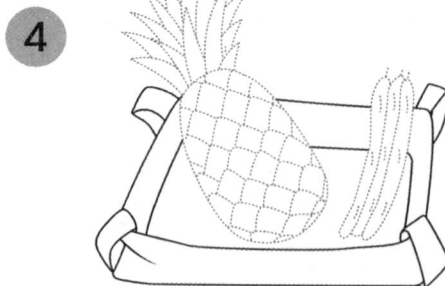

4

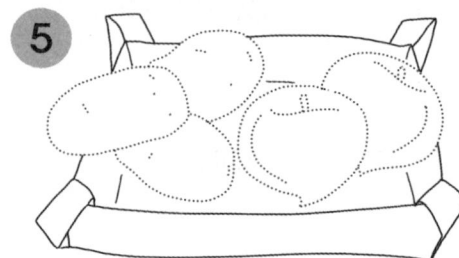

5

_____   _____   _____

_____   _____   _____

_____

1 **Look, read and write.**

> **Remember**
> a / an / some

bread   peach   grapes   apple   carrots   egg

1 Can I have _____ some bread _____, please?

2 Can I have _____, please?

3 Can I have _____?

4 Can _____?

5 _____?

6 _____?

2 **Talk Partners** **Choose and write a conversation. Act out.**

Can I have a _____, please?

Here you are.

Can I have an _____, please?

Here you are.

Can I have some _____, please?

_____.

Thank you very much.

You're welcome.

_____

After you read

1 Read and write *true* or *false*.

1 Jake and Molly buy bread and yoghurt for breakfast.　　　　　___true___

2 Jake and Molly buy potatoes and tomatoes for lunch.　　　　_____

3 A naughty parrot takes the food.　　　　　　　　　　　　_____

4 Jake and Molly see the parrot take the food.　　　　　　　_____

5 Toby rings the bell.　　　　　　　　　　　　　　　　　_____

6 Toby has got all the food for breakfast, lunch and dinner.　_____

2  What do you have for breakfast, lunch and dinner? Draw and write.

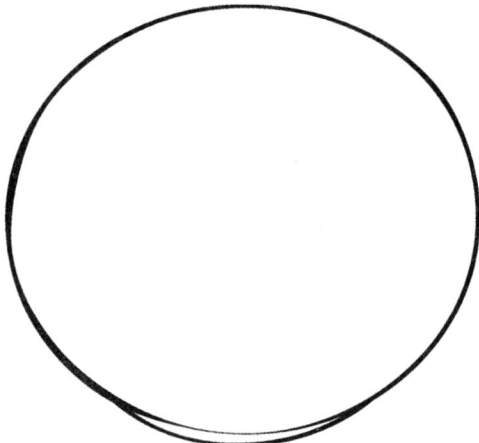

breakfast

I have

_____

_____.

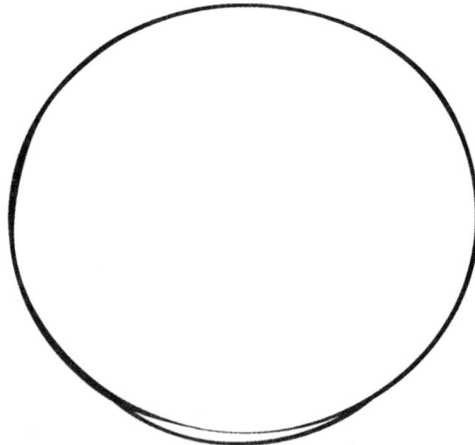

lunch

I have

_____

_____.

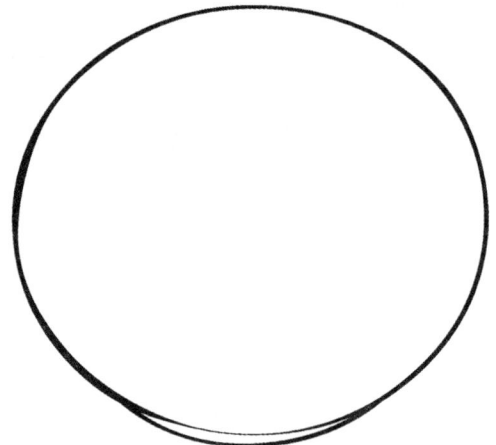

dinner

I have

_____

_____.

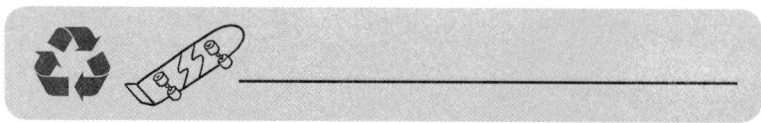

1 Listen and write the numbers. CD1 40

50 c

2 Look and write.

How much is this?   How much are these?

1 26c

How much __are these__?

They're __twenty-six__ cents.

2 32c

How much _____?

It's _____

_____.

3 47c

_____?

_____

_____.

4 39c

_____?

_____

_____.

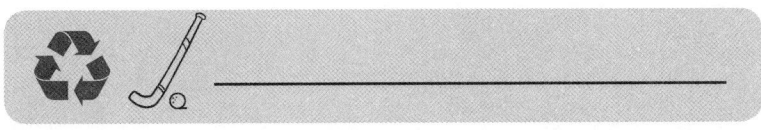

Toby's tongue twister

1 Write and say.

ee - ea. Qu_ee_n J____n ____ts m____t
and the gr____n sh____p ____ts ch____se.

2 Colour the 'ee' words red and the 'ea' words blue. Say.

sheep	meat	bee	ice cream	peach
three	sweets	peas	queen	cheese

3 💬 **Talk Partners** Play *Memory chain* in pairs.

three

three, bee

Memory chain

three, bee, peas

three, bee, peas, meat …

Play *Memory chain*: Pupils play with their Talk Partner. Pupil A chooses a word and says it. Pupil B repeats Pupil A's word and says a word of their own. Pupils take turns repeating and adding words to the chain.

1 **Listen and write. Match.**

CD1 45

| pancake | sugar | school | ~~Mum~~ | lemon |

1 I help ____Mum____ make the pancakes.

2 Mum tosses the _____ in the air.

3 I put _____ and _____
on my pancake.

4 At _____, we have pancake races.

Think about your culture

Do you have special food
in your country?

2 **Read and tick (✓). Draw, write and say.**

1 There's special food in my country. ◯

2 I eat pancakes on a special day. ◯

3 I eat cake on a special day. ◯

4 I help my mum make special food. ◯

5 I help my dad make special food. ◯

I _____.

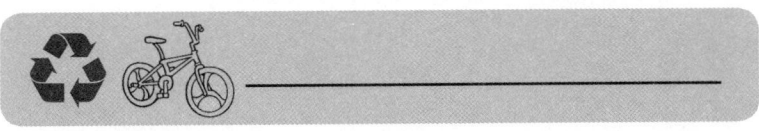

After you read

Text type: **A recipe**

1 Read and number. Match.

Then, add the eggs for eyes. Put an olive in the centre of each egg. ◯

First, put the slices of cheese on the slice of bread. ① ⎯ a

Finally, add the salad for the hair. ◯

Now, add an olive for the nose and a piece of carrot for the mouth. ◯

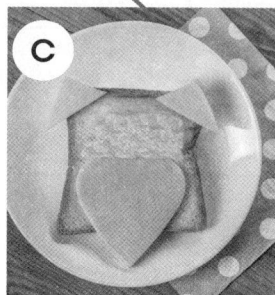

2 Choose and write your own recipe. Draw.

You need

_____bread_____   _____

_____   _____

_____   _____

banana   carrot
chocolate   cheese
egg   salad
pineapple   apple
bread   pasta

First, put the _____ on the _bread_ .

Then, add the _____ for eyes.

Now, add the _____ for the nose and the _____ for the mouth.

Finally, add the _____ for the hair.

_____

1 **Look, read and write.**

How much is this?   How much are these?

1 How much is this _____? It's ____fifty____ cents.

2 _____? They're _____ cents.

3 _____? It's _____ cents.

4 _____? _____.

5 _____? _____.

2 **Talk Partners** **Look and write. Ask and answer.**

1 Can _I have some bread, please_____?
   Yes. _Here you are_____.

2 Can _____?
   Yes. _____.

3 _____?
   _____.

4 _____?
   _____.

Remember
a peach
an orange
some bread
some carrots

3 **My progress** Use your traffic light. Listen to the teacher and point.

Key for Activity 3: **1.** I can say and write the ten food words. **2.** I can ask for different food. **3.** I can say how much food is. **4.** I can read and write a recipe. **5.** I remember to say please. **6.** I work well with my Talk Partner.

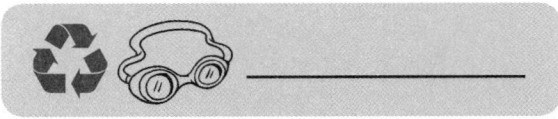

♻ 🚗 _____

Finding recipes online

1 What recipes are they making?
Listen and number.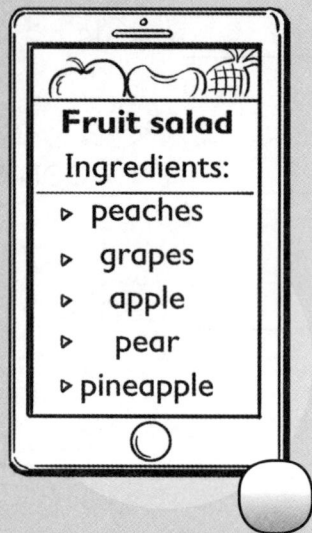
CD1 49

Pizza
Ingredients:
○ tomatoes
○ cheese
○ peppers

1

Fruit salad
Ingredients:
▷ peaches
▷ grapes
▷ apple
▷ pear
▷ pineapple

Sandwich
Ingredients:
bread
cheese
eggs
carrots
tomato

Pancakes
Ingredients:
▷ flour
▷ milk
▷ 2 eggs

21 CHANNEL

What's on your pizza?

2 Think and write. Draw your pizza.

My pizza has got

1 _____.

2 _____.

3 _____.

4 _____.

5 _____.

_____ _____

Let's practise spelling!

Look	Copy	Cover and write
1 lemons	_____	_____
2 pineapple	_____	_____
3 tomatoes	_____	_____
4 potatoes	_____	_____
5 bread	_____	_____
6 peaches	_____	_____
7 carrots	_____	_____
8 green beans	_____	_____
9 sweets	_____	_____
10 yoghurt	_____	_____

♻️ _____

Unit 3 At the zoo

1 **Look and write.**

elephant   ~~lion~~   giraffe   penguin   snake
crocodile   lizard   tiger   hippo   monkey

1   2   3   4   5

___lion___   _____   _____   _____   _____

6   7   8   9   10

_____   _____   _____   _____   _____

2 **Read and match. Write.**

I've got two legs.
I can't fly. I'm black
and white.
I'm a ___penguin___.

1

2

I've got four long
legs. I'm tall. I'm
yellow and brown.
_____.

I've got four legs.
I'm very big. I've got
big ears. I'm grey.
_____.

3

4

I've got four legs.
I'm very fat. I've got a
big mouth. I'm grey.
_____.

_____

1 **Look and tick (✓) or cross (✗). Write.**

four legs	✓			
a big mouth				
big ears				
long hair	✓			

1 A lion has got _____four legs_____ and _____long hair_____ .

2 A crocodile _____ and _____ .

3 Elephants have got _____ .

4 Hippos _____ .

2 **Talk Partners** **Write a conversation. Draw an animal. Act out.**

Can you guess my favourite animal?

Has it got _____ ?

_____ .

It's _____ .

After you read

1 Remember the story. Read and number.

This bird is very different.

Look! Here are some eggs.

Look! What's this?

I think it's an egg.

1

Look. Here's a sign.

Giraffe
• long neck
• eats leaves

Thank you for helping our lost penguin.

Wow! What is it?

2 Look, write and circle.

big ears

1 Have penguins _got big ears_____?

Yes, they have. (No, they haven't.)

feathers

2 Have penguins _____?

Yes, they have.   No, they haven't.

big teeth

3 _____?

Yes, they have.   No, they haven't.

a long neck

4 _____?

Yes, they have.   No, they haven't.

1 **What's missing? Listen and number. Write and draw.** CD2 4

| wings | teeth | a body | a face | ~~a beak~~ | a tail |

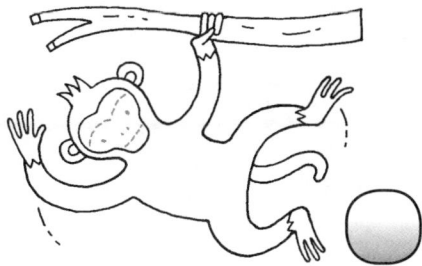  

It hasn't got _____ . It hasn't got _a beak_ . It _____ .

_____ _____ _____

_____ . _____ . _____ .

2 **What's wrong? Look and write.**

| ~~a long tail~~ | a beak | big teeth | wings |

1  They haven't got
a long tail !

2  They haven't got
_____ !

3  _____
_____ !

4 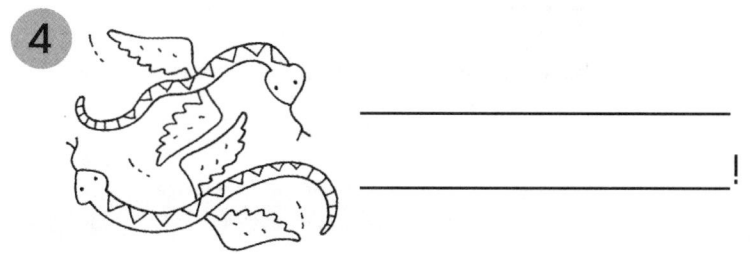 _____
_____ !

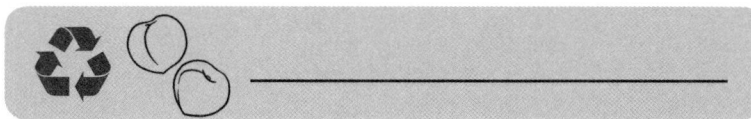 _____

Toby's tongue twister

1 Write and say.

oo – ui. A kangar _oo_ and a g____se in a swims____t drink fr____t j____ce by the p___l.

2 Colour the 'oo' words red and the 'ui' words blue. Say.

moon	kangaroo	spoon	food	swimsuit
juice	pool	fruit	balloon	zoo

3 Talk Partners Play *Snap* in pairs.

1, 2, 3 *fruit!*

1, 2, 3 *juice!*

Snap!

1, 2, 3 *moon!*

1, 2, 3 *moon!*

Snap!

Play *Snap*: Pupils play with their Talk Partner. Pupils individually think of a word, count to three together, point to the picture and say the word. If the words are the same, they say *Snap!* If they are different, they continue playing the game.

_____

1 Listen and number. Write.

CD2 9

~~birds~~   fox   hedgehogs   squirrels

1 birds

💡 **Think about your culture**

What animals can you see near your house?

2 Read and tick (✓). Draw, write and say.

1 I can see birds. ◯

2 I can see hedgehogs. ◯

3 I can see pets. ◯

4 I can see squirrels. ◯

5 I can see lizards. ◯

I _____.

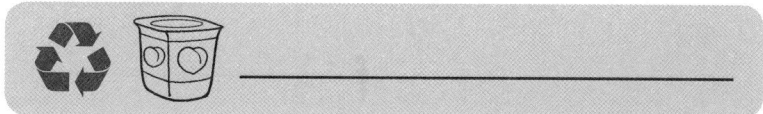

After you read

1 Read again. Write *gorillas* or *polar bears*.

1 They live in the rainforest.   *gorillas*

2 They eat fish and meat.   _____

3 They live on snow and ice.   _____

4 They've got long arms.   _____

5 They eat leaves and fruit.   _____

6 They haven't got a tail.   _____

7 They've got a small tail.   _____

8 They've got 42 teeth.   _____

2 Draw your favourite wild animal. Write a fact file.

ANIMAL FACTS

Name:

_____

Habitat:

_____

Colour:

_____

Size:

_____

Characteristics:

_____

Food:

_____

_____

1 **Look and write. Find the secret animals.**

| t | | | | |

w

secret animals:

__ __ __ __ __ and

__ __ __ __ __ __

c

m

2 **Talk Partners** Write. Ask and answer.

Has it got   Have they got

1 <u>Have they got</u> legs?   <u>No, they haven't</u>.

2 _____ a long neck?   _____.

3 _____ wings?   _____.

4 _____ a long tail?   _____.

3 **My progress** Use your traffic light. Listen to the teacher and point.

Key for Activity 3: **1.** I can say and write the ten animal words. **2.** I can ask and answer about animals. **3.** I can read and write a fact file. **4.** I can describe animals and their characteristics. **5.** I help my friends.

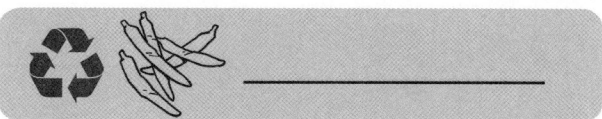

_____

1 Listen and tick (✓). CD2 13

1
✓

2

3

4

21 CHANNEL

Can you identify similarities and differences?

2 Think and write.

big teeth   long neck   tail
long legs   short legs   face

 giraffes   crocodiles

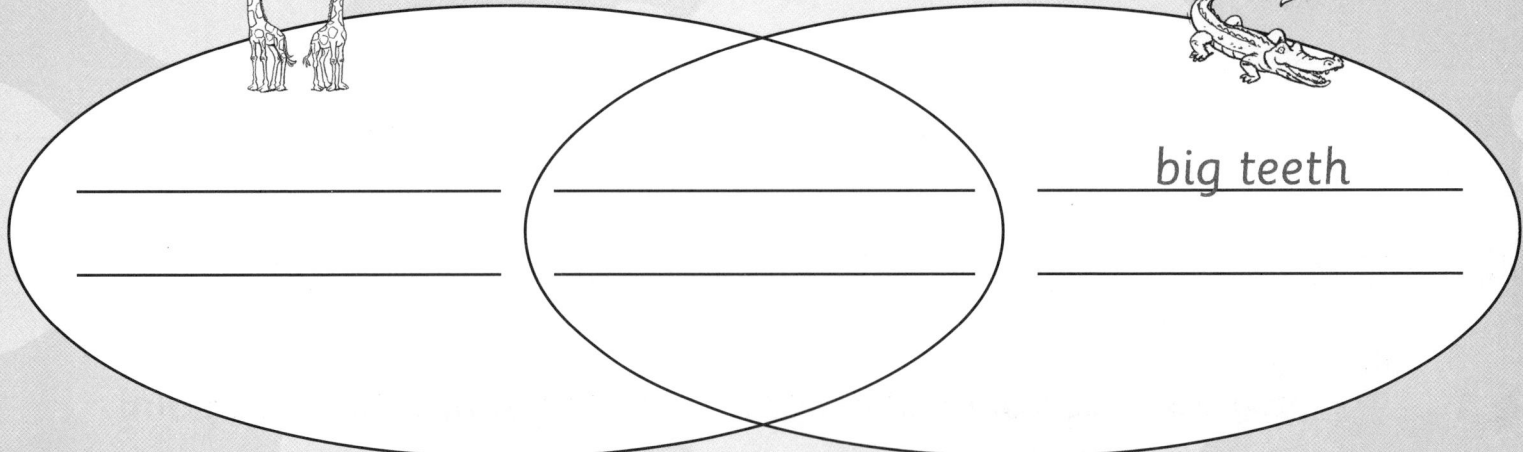

big teeth

Let's practise spelling!

	Look	Copy	Cover and write
1	crocodile	_____	_____
2	lion	_____	_____
3	elephant	_____	_____
4	penguin	_____	_____
5	tiger	_____	_____
6	lizard	_____	_____
7	snake	_____	_____
8	monkey	_____	_____
9	hippo	_____	_____
10	giraffe	_____	_____

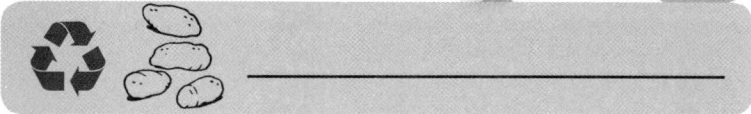

_____

Plan your project

PETS

1 Plan your pets class book page. Read, tick (✓) and write.

1 Choose a pet.

rabbit ◯   turtle ◯   hamster ◯   spider ◯

guinea pig ◯   bird ◯   goldfish ◯

stick insect ◯   cat ◯   dog ◯

2 What's its name? _____

3 What's its favourite food?

meat ◯   fish ◯   fruit ◯   vegetables ◯

4 What's its favourite toy?

a ball ◯   a wheel ◯   other: _____

5 What does your pet look like?

colour: _____

legs: zero ◯   two ◯   four ◯   six ◯   eight ◯

hair: no hair ◯   long hair ◯   short hair ◯

6 Where does it live?

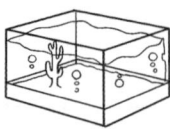   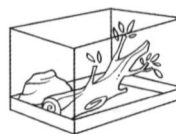   

in water ◯   in a cage ◯   in a tank ◯   in a house ◯

1 **Plan your pets class book page.**

This is my _____.

Its name is _____.

Its favourite food is _____.

Its favourite toy is _____.

It's _____.

It's got _____ legs and _____ hair.

It lives in _____.

Think about your project

2 **Read, think and colour the stars.**

I listen to my friends.

I share my things.

I help my friends.

I make an effort.

I like the display.

Unit 4 The nature trail

1 **Read and match.**

1 I can walk in the forest.

2 I can jump in the leaves.

3 I can climb the hill.

4 I can swim in the lake.

5 I can play in the sand.

6 I can run in the grass.

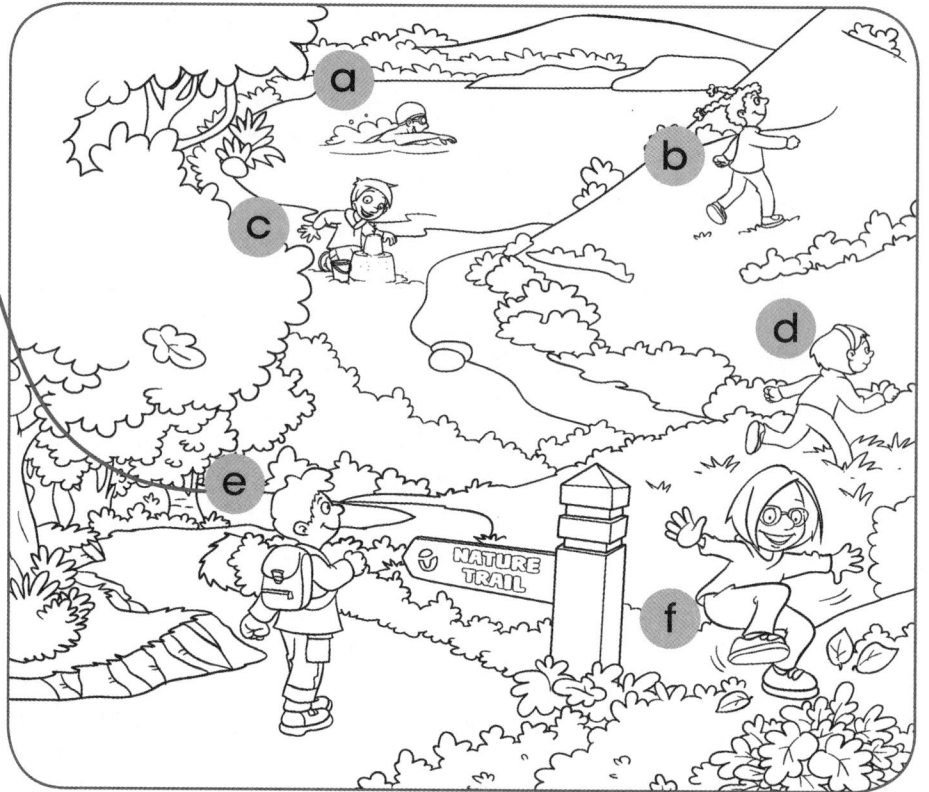

2 **Look, read and write.**

forest   grass   hill   river   ~~path~~   bridge   road   leaves   sand   lake

1   2   3   4   5

path _____ _____ _____ _____

         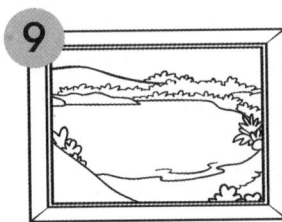   

6   7   8   9   10

_____ _____ _____ _____ _____

_____

1 **Look and write.**

swimming playing walking climbing jumping	bridge leaves sand forest lake

1 I'm  _____swimming_____ in the 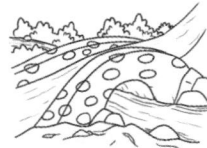 _____.

2 I'm  _____ on the  _____.

3 I'm  _____ in the  _____.

4 I'm  _____ in the  _____.

5 I'm _____ _____ in the _____ _____.

2 **Talk Partners** Write a conversation. Draw. Act out.

What are you _____?

Can you guess?

Are _____?

Yes, _____.

4 Lesson 3 Story

After you read

1 Remember the story. Read and number.

He's chasing the sheep. ◯

He's rolling down the hill. ◯

He's running in the flowers. ◯

He's jumping in the lake. ◯

He's running up the hill. ◯

That's better! ⑧

Toby has got something in his nose. ◯

Let's go on the nature trail! ①

2 Talk Partners Help Toby to cross the river. Join with different colours. Say.

running

jumping

climbing

Toby is

walking

playing

swimming

in

the

leaves

forest

lake

grass

flowers

sand

1 Listen and write. Match. CD2 27

across   up   down   along   across

1 He's riding a horse ___across___ the sand.

2 She's walking _____ the hill.

3 He's running _____ the hill.

4 She's riding a bike _____ the road.

5 She's swimming _____ the lake.

2 Read, look and write.

No, he isn't.   Yes, he is.   Yes, she is.   No, she isn't.   Yes, she is.

1 Is he walking up a hill?

___Yes, he is___.

2 Is she running along a path?

_____.

3 Is she running down a hill?

_____.

4 Is she riding a horse in the forest?

_____.

5 Is he swimming in the lake?

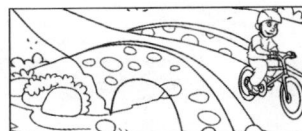

_____.

 _____

Toby's tongue twister

1   **Write and say.**

or – **al**. The h_ or _se in sh___ts w___ks and t___ks in a st___m.

2   **Colour the 'or' words red and the 'al' words blue. Say.**

horse	chalk	shorts	storm	fork
short	walk	sport	talk	corn

3   💬 **Talk Partners** Play *Memory chain* in pairs.

horse

horse, walk

Memory chain

horse, walk, storm

horse, walk, storm, talk …

Play *Memory chain*: Pupils play with their Talk Partner. Pupil A chooses a word and says it. Pupil B repeats Pupil A's word and says a word of their own. Pupils take turns repeating and adding words to the chain.

1 **Listen and tick (✓).** CD2 31

1 We make a den from …

branches. ✓　　stones. ○　　twigs. ○　　rocks. ○　　leaves. ○

2 We decorate mud pies with …

sweets. ○　　leaves. ○　　stones. ○　　chocolate. ○　　flowers. ○

3 We go on a minibeast hunt. We see …

caterpillars. ○　　elephants. ○　　butterflies. ○　　sheep. ○　　worms. ○

Think about your culture

What do you do in the forest?

2 **Read and tick (✓). Draw, write and say.**

1 I walk. ○

2 I make a den from branches, twigs and leaves. ○

3 I take photos. ○

4 I make mud pies. ○

5 I count the animals. ○

I _____.

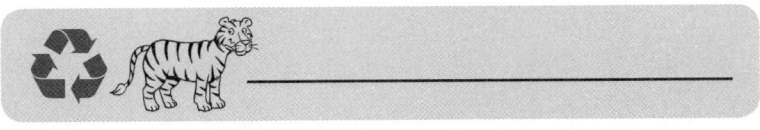

_____

After you read

Text type: **An adventure story**

1 **Read and number.**

1 Mummies chase Adam.

2 He sails across the lake.

3 He goes along the secret passage.

4 He crosses the old rope bridge.

5 He finds the treasure.

6 The spiders run away.

1

2 **Choose and write an adventure story.**

1 sails across the ...   river   lake   pool

2 walks across the ...   grass   bridge   sand

3 goes along the ...   path   road   secret passage

4 sees the ...   monkeys   mummies   monsters

5 finds the ...   map   treasure   key

Adam is playing in the park. He finds a map in the grass .

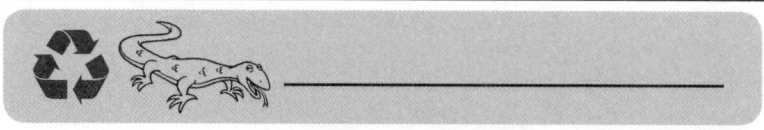

He .

.

.

1 🗨 **Talk Partners** Play the game. Throw the dice. Ask and answer.

What's he doing? He's jumping in the leaves.

2 **Look at the game. Choose and write.**

1 She's <u>running down a hill</u> .

2 He's _____ .

3 _____ .

4 _____ .

Remember
he's/she's run**ning**
he's/she's swim**ming**

3 **My progress** Use your traffic light. Listen to the teacher and point.

Key for Activity 3: 1. I can say and write the ten nature trail words. **2.** I can ask and answer about actions people are doing. **3.** I can read and write an adventure story. **4.** I can sing a song. **5.** I work well with my Talk Partner.

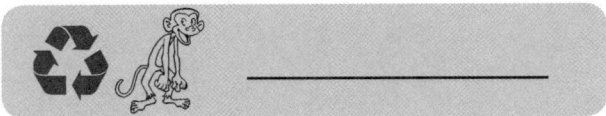

1 Read, listen and match. Write. CD2 36

a

1 I walk on the path in the

_____forest_____.

b

2 I don't feed wild animals at the

_____.

3 I respect the signs in the

_____.

c

4 I put my rubbish in the bin at the

_____.

d

21 CHANNEL

What do you do to look after
the environment?

2 me Read and tick (✓). Draw a sign.

1 I put my rubbish in the bin. ◯

2 I walk on the path. ◯

3 I don't feed wild animals. ◯

4 I respect the signs. ◯

5 I don't touch wild flowers. ◯

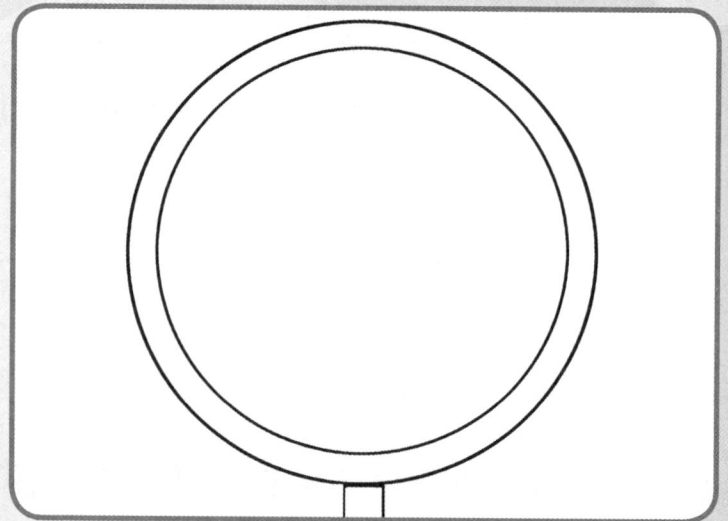

♻ two _____

Let's practise spelling!

Look	Copy	Cover and write
1 road	_____	_____
2 hill	_____	_____
3 bridge	_____	_____
4 lake	_____	_____
5 sand	_____	_____
6 leaves	_____	_____
7 river	_____	_____
8 path	_____	_____
9 forest	_____	_____
10 grass	_____	_____

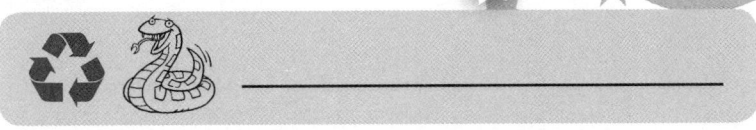

♻️ 🐍 _____

The frozen lake

1 Look, read and circle.

1. We're (skating.) / drinking.

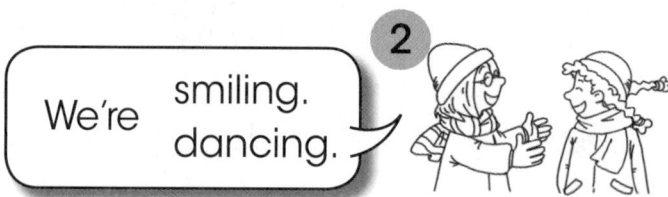

2. We're smiling. / dancing.

3. We're making a snowman. / listening to music.

4. We're playing. / waving.

5. We're drinking. / eating.

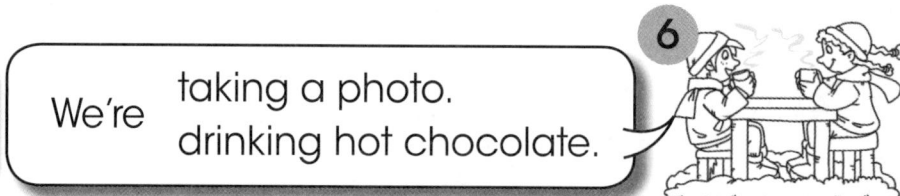

6. We're taking a photo. / drinking hot chocolate.

2 Look, read and write.

skating   dancing   drinking   listening   playing   taking

1 We're ___skating___ on the ice.

2 We're _____.

3 We're _____ to music.

4 We're _____ hot chocolate.

5 We're _____ a photo.

6 We're _____.

1 **Look and write.**

eating   dancing   skating   ~~smiling~~   drinking   taking a photo

1 What <u>are you doing</u> ?  We're <u>smiling</u>.

2 What _____ ?  We're _____.

3 _____ ?  _____.

4 _____ ?  _____.

5 _____ ?  _____.

6 _____ ?  _____.

2 **Talk Partners** **Write about you and a friend. Draw. Act out.**

Are you _____ ?

No, we aren't.

Are _____ ?

Yes, we are. Look!

_____

After you read

1 Remember the story. Number and write.

park   hill   arms   snowman   ~~tummy~~   taking

Let's go to the _____!

These are his _____.

Look! He's got a fat _tummy_.

They go sledging down the _____.

He's _____ the magic bike.

Look at the _____. He's moving.

2 What happens next in the story? Tick (✓) and draw.

1 They take a photo. ◯

2 They go to the park. ◯

3 They skate on the ice. ◯

4 They _____. ◯

 _____

1 Listen and tick (✓). Write.

CD2 46

clean   fat   ~~tall~~   dirty   clean   fat

1

He's a _____tall_____ snowman.

2

He's got a _____ tummy.

3

He's got a _____ scarf
and a _____ hat.

4

He's got a _____ tummy
and a _____ hat.

2 Choose and write. Draw a snowman.

tall   fat   thin   short
dirty   clean   big

scarf   snowman   arms
nose   hat   tummy

1 He's a _____ snowman.

2 He's got a _____ .

3 He's got a _____
and _____ .

Toby's tongue twister

1 **Write and say.**

ow – oa. A sn __ow__ man and a g___t in a c___t r___ a yell___ b___t to the rainb___.

2 **Colour the 'ow' words red and the 'oa' words blue. Say.**

snow	road	toad	window	slow
soap	coat	rainbow	boat	goat

3 **Talk Partners** Play *Snap* in pairs.

1, 2, 3 snow!

1, 2, 3 boat!

Snap!

1, 2, 3 coat!

1, 2, 3 coat!

Snap!

Play Snap: Pupils play with their Talk Partner. Pupils individually think of a word, count to three together, point to the picture and say the word. If the words are the same, they say *Snap!* If they are different, they continue playing the game.

1 Listen and number. Write.
CD2 51

skiing   skating   tubing   riding

1

They're ___skiing___ on a dry ski slope.

_____ on the ice rink.

They're _____ down a hill.

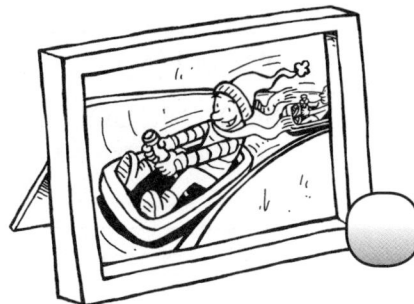

They're _____ on a toboggan.

Think about your culture

What winter activities do you do?

2 Read and tick (✓). Draw, write and say.

1 I ride on a toboggan. ⬭

2 I go skiing. ⬭

3 I go ice skating. ⬭

4 I go tubing. ⬭

5 I make a snowman. ⬭

I _____.

_____

fifty-three **53**

After you read

Text type: **A fable**

1 Read, number and match.

We're working. We're collecting food for winter. ◯

Can I have some food? ◯

Hello, ants! What are you doing? ①

a   b

No. Go and look for food in the snow! ◯

Come and play. ◯

Winter is coming. ◯

2 Write the conversations. Draw.

It's summer.

Hello, ants! What _____?

We_____.

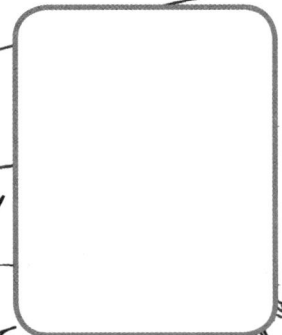

It's winter.

I'm hungry! Can _____?

_____.

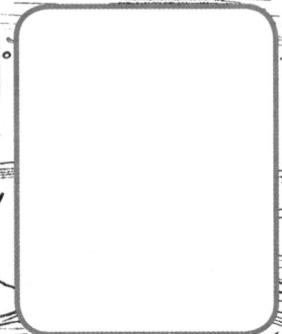

_____

1 Find, circle and write.

S	N	S	H	O	R	T	O	W
N	N	E	W	M	F	A	T	A
T	A	L	L	B	F	A	S	T
I	O	L	D	D	I	R	T	Y
F	G	A	T	H	I	N	T	A
S	H	P	L	T	S	L	S	W
C	L	E	A	N	R	S	A	G

1 a ___clean___ snowman

2 a _____

3 _____

4 _____

5 _____

6 _____

2 Order the sentences.

taking | They're | a | photo

1 They're _____.

listening | music | We're | to

2 _____.

making | They're | a | snowman

3 _____.

drinking | chocolate | hot | We're

4 _____.

3 My progress Use your traffic light. Listen to the teacher and point.

Key for Activity 3: 1. I can say and write the ten action words. 2. I can ask and answer about actions people are doing. 3. I can read a fable. 4. I can understand a moral. 5. I work well with my Talk Partner.

_____

Being creative

1 Listen and number. CD2 56

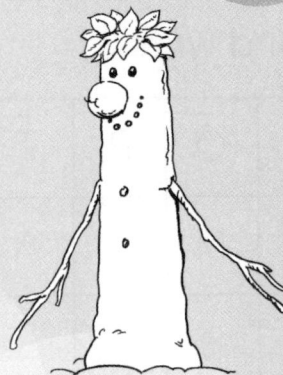 1

 **CHANNEL**

What's your snowman like?

2 Think and write. Draw your snowman.

My snowman is

_____

and _____.

It's got _____.

It's got _____.

and _____.

Let's practise spelling!

Look	Copy	Cover and write
1 dance	_____	_____
2 smile	_____	_____
3 skate	_____	_____
4 take a photo	_____	_____
5 eat	_____	_____
6 drink	_____	_____
7 listen to music	_____	_____
8 make a snowman	_____	_____
9 play	_____	_____
10 wave	_____	_____

_____

All year round

1 **Read and circle.**

1 We finish school in …   autumn.   (summer.)

2 We plant seeds in …   summer.   spring.

3 We open presents in …   winter.   summer.

4 We smell flowers in …   autumn.   spring.

5 We wear warm clothes in …   summer.   winter.

6 We eat chestnuts in …   autumn.   spring.

2 **Look and write.**

~~plant seeds~~   wear warm clothes   go to the beach   celebrate Halloween

1 We _____plant seeds_____ in spring.

2 We _____ in summer.

3 We _____ in autumn.

4 We _____ in winter.

1 What do Beth, Molly and Jake do? Match and write.

1 plant seeds

2 celebrate Halloween

3 go to the beach

4 open presents

winter   spring   summer   autumn

1 They _____ in ___*spring*___.

2 They _____.

3 _____.

4 _____.

2 **Talk Partners** Think about your family. Write and draw. Act out.

What do you do in _____?

We _____.

Do you _____?

_____.

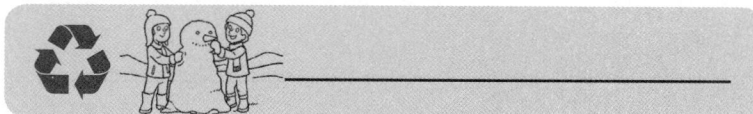

6 Lesson 3 **Story**

After you read

1 Remember the story. Read and number.

It's summer now. ◯

We've got lots of photos for our projects now. ◯

We can help you. ◯

Do you eat chestnuts in America, too? ◯

It's spring. I can smell flowers. ◯

We're doing a project about the seasons. ①

2 Write and draw.

summer ~~spring~~ winter autumn

1 __spring__	2 _____	3 _____	4 _____
Flowers grow.	The tree has got green leaves.	There are chestnuts on the tree.	The tree hasn't got leaves.

_____

1 Listen and circle. CD3 10

1 May

1	2	3	4	5	6	7
8	9	10	11	12	13	(14)
15	16	17	18	19	20	21
22	23	24	25	26	27	28
29	30	31				

2 August

			1	2	3	4
5	6	7	8	9	10	11
12	13	14	15	16	17	18
19	20	21	22	23	24	25
26	27	28	29	30	31	

3 October

1	2	3	4	5	6	7
8	9	10	11	12	13	14
15	16	17	18	19	20	21
22	23	24	25	26	27	28
29	30	31				

4 January

		1	2	3	4	5
6	7	8	9	10	11	12
13	14	15	16	17	18	19
20	21	22	23	24	25	26
27	28	29	30	31		

2 When's your birthday? Read and write.

My birthday is on the _____ of _____.

3 Find, circle and write.

A	R	T	W	E	L	F	T	H	M
H	F	O	U	R	T	H	T	N	O
S	O	F	T	F	I	R	S	T	O
H	S	E	V	E	N	T	H	R	N
T	E	N	T	H	S	I	X	T	H
A	E	Y	E	T	H	I	R	D	E
N	I	N	T	H	F	I	F	T	H
E	L	E	V	E	N	T	H	T	O
E	E	I	G	H	T	H	W	T	R
N	S	E	C	O	N	D	H	F	E

1st _____ first
2nd _____
3rd _____
4th _____
5th _____
6th _____
7th _____
8th _____
9th _____
10th _____
11th _____
12th _____

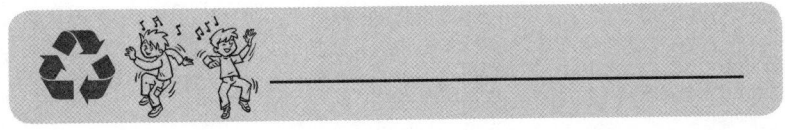

_____

1 Write and say.

ur – **ir**. Is the p_ur_ple t___tle's b___rthday on the f___st or the th___d?

2 Colour the 'ur' words red and the 'ir' words blue. Say.

turtle	shirt	thirty	turn	nurse
bird	girl	first	surf	Thursday

3 **Talk Partners** Play *Memory chain* in pairs.

shirt

shirt, turtle

Memory chain

shirt, turtle, surf

shirt, turtle, surf, bird ...

Play *Memory chain*: Pupils play with their Talk Partner. Pupil A chooses a word and says it. Pupil B repeats Pupil A's word and says a word of their own. Pupils take turns repeating and adding words to the chain.

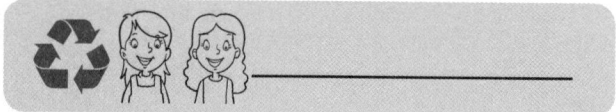

1 **Look, read and match.**

1 AUGUST

2 DECEMBER 25th

3 NOVEMBER 5th

4 APRIL 1st

CHRISTMAS DAY

CARNIVAL

APRIL FOOLS' DAY

BONFIRE NIGHT

a

b

c

d

💡 **Think about your culture**

What do you do on festival days?

2 **Read and tick (✓). Draw, write and say.**

1 We play jokes on the first of April. ◯

2 We eat Christmas dinner on the twenty-fourth of December. ◯

3 We have a bonfire in November. ◯

4 We play jokes in December. ◯

5 We have Carnival in February. ◯

We _____.

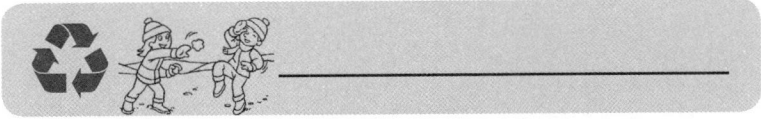

After you read

Text type: **A traditional rhyme**

1 Read and number.

April, June and November. ◯

And that has twenty-eight days clear, ◯

There are thirty days in September, ①

Except for February alone. ◯

And twenty-nine in each leap year! ◯

All the rest have thirty-one, ◯

2 **Talk Partners** Write the missing words. Say the rhyme.

thirty-one   twenty-nine   February   June   ~~September~~   April   November

There are thirty days in ___September___,

_____, _____ and _____.

All the rest have _____,

Except for _____ alone.

And that has twenty-eight days clear,

And _____ in each leap year!

1 **Listen and write the date.**
CD3 18

twenty-seventh   tenth   ~~twenty-fifth~~   eighth

1

twenty-fifth of December

2

_____

3

_____

4

_____

2 💬 **Talk Partners** **Look and write. Ask and answer.**

1

What do they do _____ in winter?

They _____.

2

_____ in summer?

_____.

3

_____ in autumn?

_____.

4

_____ in spring?

_____.

3 **My progress** **Use your traffic light. Listen to the teacher and point.**

Key for Activity 3: 1. I can say and write the activities we do each season. 2. I can ask and answer about birthdays. 3. I can read a traditional rhyme. 4. I know about seasonal festivals in Britain. 5. I work well with my Talk Partner.

♻ _____

1 Listen and tick (✓). CD3 19

1

| 15th February | 5th May ✓ |

3

| 14th July | 14th August |

2

| 19th December | 17th December |

4

| 9th November | 20th October |

21 CHANNEL

When's your birthday? What season is it in?

2 Do a survey. Ask your friends and write.

Name	Birthday	Season

Let's practise spelling!

Look	Copy	Cover and write
1  plant seeds		
2  smell flowers		
3  finish school		
4  go to the beach		
5  eat chestnuts		
6  celebrate Halloween		
7  wear warm clothes		
8 open presents		

 _____

Plan your project

JOBS

1 Plan your jobs poster. Read, discuss and write.

1 Choose a job for your poster.

Our poster is about _____.

2 What does he / she wear? Tick (✓).

a uniform ◯   a helmet ◯   a hat ◯

a white coat ◯   shorts and a T-shirt ◯   a dress ◯

boots ◯   a shirt and trousers ◯

3 What does he / she do? Tick (✓).

dances ◯   plays football ◯   paints pictures ◯

cooks ◯   puts out fires ◯   teaches children ◯

flies a plane ◯   helps people ◯   helps animals ◯

4 Choose *He* or *She*. Write.

_____ is _____.

_____ wears _____.

_____.

Remember
a / an + job

1 **Look at the class jobs wall display. Read and write.**

1 There are _____ different jobs on the class jobs wall.

2 There are a lot of posters about _____.

3 There aren't posters about _____.

4 _____ jobs have got a uniform.

5 My favourite jobs poster is about _____.

Think about your project

2 **Read, think and colour the stars.**

I listen to my friends.

I share my things.

I help my friends.

I make an effort.

I like the display.

Unit 7 **My house**

1 Read and match. Say.

1 There's a mouse
watching TV in the …

2 There's a mouse
having a shower in the …

3 There's a mouse
eating all the food in the …

4 There's a mouse
running on the floor in the …

5 There's a mouse
watering the flowers in the …

living room.

garden.

bathroom.

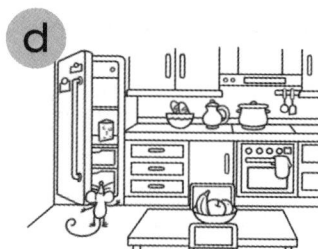
kitchen.

garage.

2 Look and write. Find the secret word.

flat   living room   kitchen   bedroom   hall
dining room   house   garage   bathroom

secret word:
— — — — — — —

h

b

l

d

1 **Write and match.**

There's   There are

 a   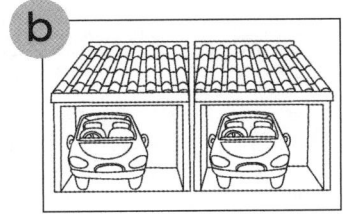 b

1 _____There's_____ a big kitchen.

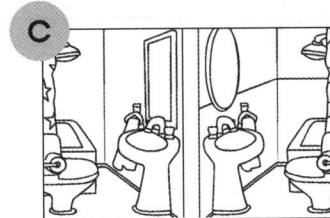 c    d

2 _____ two small bedrooms.

3 _____ two bathrooms.

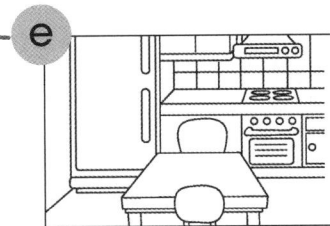 e    f

4 _____ a living room.

5 _____ two garages.

6 _____ a dining room.

2 **Order and write. Number.**

1

the	isn't	a
~~There~~	kitchen	
in	shower	

There _____

_____.

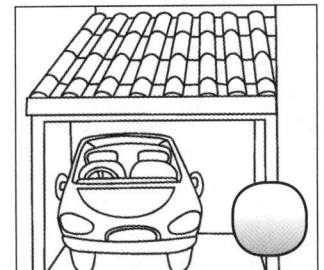

2

There	the
any	aren't	in
garden	chairs

_____

_____.

3

a	garage
in	There	sofa
isn't	the

_____

_____.

_____

After you read

1 Remember the story. Read, look and write.

| dining room | bedroom | bathroom | ~~living room~~ |

| ~~sofa~~ | bath | armchair | bed | mirror | piano | shower |

There's a haunted <u>living room</u> with a haunted _____ <u>sofa</u>

and a haunted _____. There's a haunted _____

with a haunted _____ and a haunted _____.

There's a haunted _____ with a haunted _____

and a haunted _____. There's a haunted _____

with a haunted _____.

2 Read and write. Draw a haunted house.

1 There's a _____
   with a haunted _____.

2 There are _____
   with a haunted _____.

3 There isn't _____
   _____.

4 There aren't any _____
   _____.

_____

1   **Look, read and write. Listen and check.**

CD3 33

~~radio~~   camera   box   clock   phone   ~~mine~~   yours   his   hers   mine

1  Whose is this _____radio_____?   It's _____mine_____.

2  Whose is this _____?   It's _____.

3  Whose is _____?   It's _____.

4  Whose _____?   _____.

5  _____?   _____.

2   **Find and colour. Write.**

r_____

c_____

c_____

b_____

w_____

p_____

_____

Toby's tongue twister

1 Write and say.

ow – ou. A br_ow_n c____ and a l____d m____se run ar____nd the h____se.

2 Colour the 'ow' words red and the 'ou' words blue. Say.

mouse	mouth	cow	count	cloud
clown	house	crown	owl	shower

3 💬 **Talk Partners** Play *Snap* in pairs.

1, 2, 3 cow!

1, 2, 3 mouse!

Snap!

1, 2, 3 count!

1, 2, 3 count!

Snap!

Play Snap: Pupils play with their Talk Partner. Pupils individually think of a word, count to three together, point to the picture and say the word. If the words are the same, they say *Snap!* If they are different, they continue playing the game.

1 **Listen and match. Look and write.**

CD3 37

board games   bookcase   sticker collection   radio

1 Alex

a  _____

2 Kim

b  *board games*

3 Jill

c  _____

4 Ben

d  _____

Think about your culture

What do you do in your bedroom?

2 **Read and tick (✓). Draw, write and say.**

1 I listen to pop music. ◯

2 I play games. ◯

3 I read books. ◯

4 I play the guitar. ◯

5 I have a pyjama party. ◯

I _____.

 _____

After you read

Text type: **A play script**

1 Read again and circle.

1 Cinderella lives in a **flat** / **house**.

2 There are **sixteen** / **seventeen** bathrooms.

3 Cinderella's dress is **old** / **new**.

4 Cinderella's new dress is **purple** / **blue**.

5 The fairy godmother turns the mice into **cows** / **horses**.

6 Cinderella goes **swimming** / **dancing**.

7 She loses her **phone** / **shoe**.

8 The shoes are made of **paper** / **glass**.

2 **Talk Partners** Write the conversations. Act out.

1

Whose is this _phone_ ?

It's _____.

2

Do you want to _____?

_____.

3

_____?

_____.

4

Cinderella. Is it _____?

Yes, _____.
Thank you!

_____

1 **Follow and write.**

1 📷 ——— mine

2 📱 ——— yours

3 🎁 ——— his

4 ⌚ ——— hers

1 Whose is this camera?
It's _____ _hers_ _____.

2 Whose _____?
It's _____.

3 _____?
_____.

4 _____?
_____.

2 💬 **Talk Partners** **Play the** *House* **game. Throw the dice and say.**

There's a box in the living room.   There isn't a radio in the bathroom.

START   FINISH

3 **My progress** **Use your traffic light. Listen to the teacher and point.**

Key for Activity 3: 1. I can say and write the rooms of the house. 2. I can talk about my house. 3. I can read a play script. 4. I can ask and answer about personal objects. 5. I listen to the teacher.

seventy-seven 77

1 Where do these things go? Listen and match. CD3 41

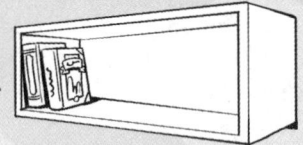
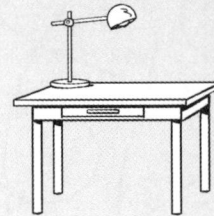

What do you do to help at home?

2 Read and tick (✓). Draw and say.

1 I tidy up. ◯

2 I make my bed. ◯

3 I clean the car. ◯

4 I water the plants. ◯

5 I make my breakfast. ◯

6 I _____.

 _____

Let's practise spelling!

	Look	Copy	Cover and write
1	house	_____	_____
2	flat	_____	_____
3	bedroom	_____	_____
4	kitchen	_____	_____
5	living room	_____	_____
6	dining room	_____	_____
7	hall	_____	_____
8	garden	_____	_____
9	garage	_____	_____
10	bathroom	_____	_____

_____   _____

1 Read and match.

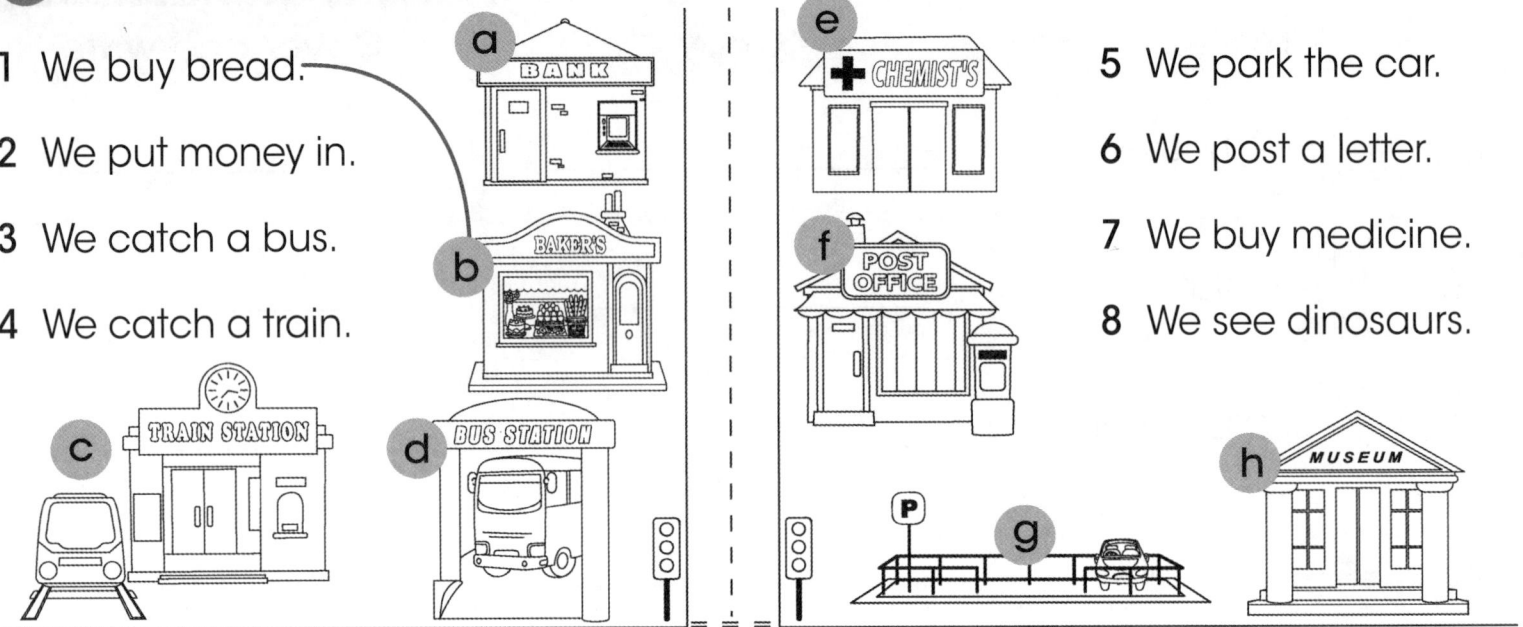

1 We buy bread.

2 We put money in.

3 We catch a bus.

4 We catch a train.

a BANK

b BAKER'S

c TRAIN STATION

d BUS STATION

e CHEMIST'S

f POST OFFICE

g

h MUSEUM

5 We park the car.

6 We post a letter.

7 We buy medicine.

8 We see dinosaurs.

2 Read, look and write.

1 It's behind the post office.   car park

2 It's in front of the police station. _____

3 It's next to the fire station.   _____

4 It's between the bank and the baker's. _____

5 It's in front of the museum.   _____

1 💬 **Talk Partners** Look and write. Ask and answer.

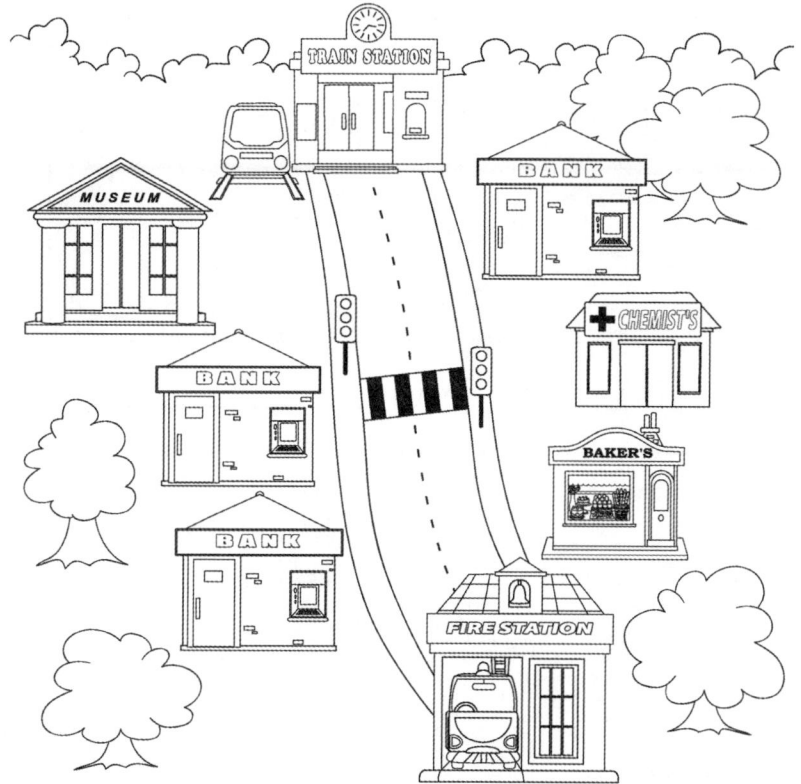

1 Is there a train station?

Yes, <u>there is</u>_____.

2 <u>Are there</u>_____ any banks?

Yes, _____.

3 _____ post office?

_____.

4 _____ car parks?

_____.

5 _____ fire station?

_____.

2 🧑‍🦱(me) **Order.** Think about your town and write.

1

there Is a
museum

<u>Is there</u>_____? _____.

2

any chemist's
Are there

_____? _____.

3

station there
Is a police

_____? _____.

4

train Are any
stations there

_____? _____.

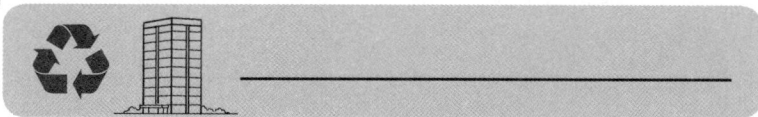

After you read

1 Remember the story. Number and write.

baker's   post office   cinema   ~~bank~~   chemist's

_____bank_____ and _____   _____

_____   _____

2 **Talk Partners** Think about the story and write. Ask and answer.

Story Quiz

1 Is there a _____ in the story?

2 Are there any _____ in the story?

3 _____ in the story?

4 _____ in the story?

Score

1 **Read and match. Listen and number.** CD3 51

Go straight on.

Turn right.

Turn left.

 a

 b

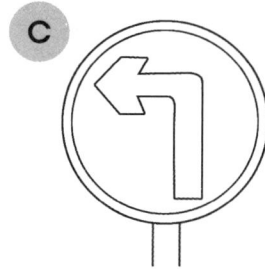 c

2 **Talk Partners** **Look and write. Say.**

turn left   turn right   go straight on   There's the fire station.

How do I get from the museum to the fire station?

_____

_____

_____

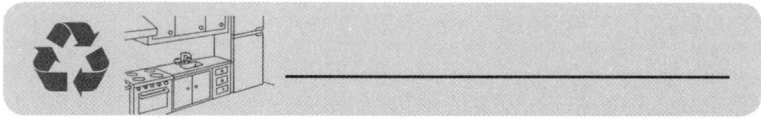

_____

Toby's tongue twister

1 Write and say.

y - **igh**. Can a fly___ with a l___t fl___ at n___t?

2 Colour the 'y' words blue and the 'igh' words red. Say.

sky

night

right

dry

light

fight

cry

fly

3 💬 **Talk Partners** Play *Memory chain* in pairs.

fly

fly, night

Memory chain

fly, night, cry

fly, night, cry, dry …

<u>Play *Memory chain*</u>: Pupils play with their Talk Partner. Pupil A chooses a word and says it. Pupil B repeats Pupil A's word and says a word of their own. Pupils take turns repeating and adding words to the chain.

1   **Read and write. Listen and check.**

CD4 4

| helmet | bike | ~~fire engine~~ | wheels | 999 | jacket | uniform | helmet |

Firefighters drive a _fire engine_ .

It's got big _____ and a loud

siren. Police officers ride a _____.

They wear a yellow _____

and a cycling _____.

Firefighters wear a safety _____

and a yellow _____.

The emergency number is _____.

💡 **Think about your culture**

> What are firefighters and police officers like in your country?

2    **Read and tick (✓). Draw, write and say.**

1   Firefighters drive a big, red fire engine. ◯

2   There are women police officers in my country. ◯

3   Firefighters wear a yellow helmet. ◯

4   The emergency number is 112. ◯

5   Police officers ride a bike. ◯

_____

_____ .

 ♻ _____

8 Lesson 7 **Literacy**

After you read

Text type: **An invitation**

1 Read again. Write.

1 Who's the invitation for? _____Jane_____

2 Who's the invitation from? _____

3 When's the party? _____

4 Where's the party? _____

5 What's Sam's telephone number? _____

2 Write an invitation. Draw.

It's party time!

To: ....

Come to my party on

....

From ....

There's ....

....

Phone number: ....

See you there!

The party is at

....

From the school:

....

....

....

....

....

1 me 💬 **Talk Partners** Write about your street. Ask and answer.

1 Are there any _____ _____baker's_____ ? _____.

2 Is there a _____ _____ ? _____.

3 Are _____ _____ _____ ? _____.

4 _____ _____ _____ ? _____.

5 _____ _____ _____ ? _____.

2 💬 **Talk Partners** Look at the map. Write. Ask and answer.

1
How do I get from the **a** _____fire_____
_____station_____ to the **d** _____
_____?

Go _____.
Turn _____.

2
How _____
b _____
c _____ ?

_____.
_____.

3 **My progress** Use your traffic light. Listen to the teacher and point.

Key for Activity 3: **1.** I can say and write the ten places in town. **2.** I can ask and answer about places. **3.** I can ask for and give directions. **4.** I can read an invitation. **5.** I can complete an invitation.

♻ _____

Crossing the road safely

1 Listen and number. CD4 9

I wait for the green man.

I look and listen. 1

I walk across the road.

I look for a zebra crossing.

21 CHANNEL

What do you do to cross the road safely?

2 me Read, think and write. Draw and say.

1 I walk across the _____.

2 I wait for the _____ man.

3 I look and _____ when I

cross the road.

4 I look for a _____ crossing.

_____

Let's practise spelling!

Look	Copy	Cover and write
1 baker's	_____	_____
2 bank	_____	_____
3 chemist's	_____	_____
4 museum	_____	_____
5 train station	_____	_____
6 bus station	_____	_____
7 car park	_____	_____
8 police station	_____	_____
9 fire station	_____	_____
10 post office	_____	_____

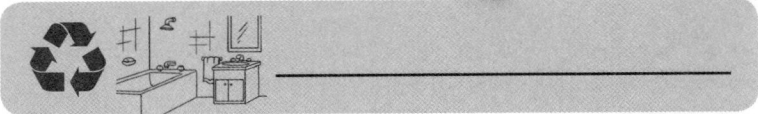

_____

Unit 9 Holiday fun

1 Read and match.

1 Let's go to the aquarium ⎯⎯⎯⎯⎯ to see fish.

2 Let's go to the water park — to see a play.

3 Let's go to the chocolate factory — to play sport.

4 Let's go to the sports centre — to make chocolate.

5 Let's go to the theatre — to play on the slides.

2 Look and write.

safari park   castle   circus   funfair   science museum   ~~water park~~

1
water park

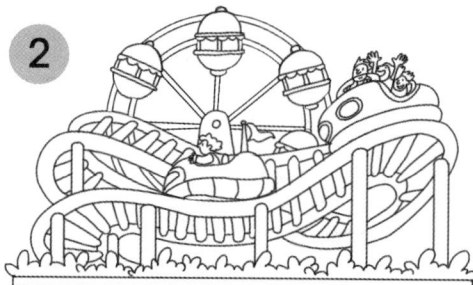
2

3

4

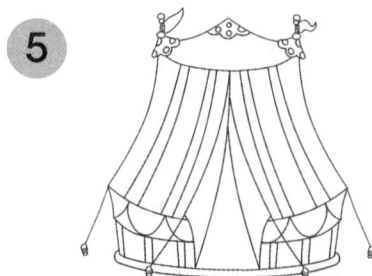
5

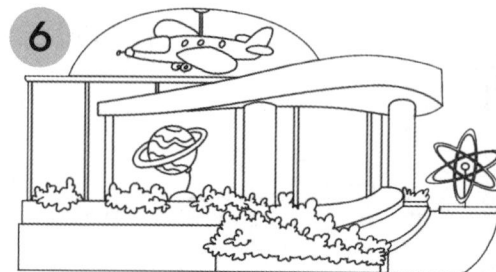
6

1 **Where were they yesterday? Look and write.**

aquarium   castle   ~~funfair~~   safari park   theatre   circus

1 I was at the _funfair_.

2 I _____.

3 _____.

4 _____.

5 _____.

6 _____.

2 **Where were you yesterday? Write and draw.**

Yesterday, _____

_____

_____

_____.

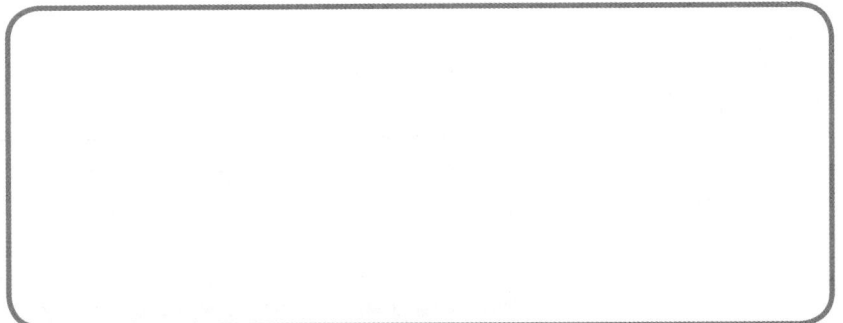

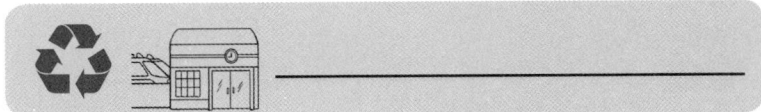

After you read

1 **Remember the story. Write *true* or *false*.**

1 It's the summer holidays.   _____true_____

2 The magic bike can fly.   _____

3 The children go to the castle first.   _____

4 They go to the aquarium.   _____

5 Molly wants to go to the funfair.   _____

6 They go to the chocolate factory.   _____

2 **Remember the story. Look and write.**

1 Where were you?

   I was _____.

2 Where _____?

   _____.

3 _____?

   _____.

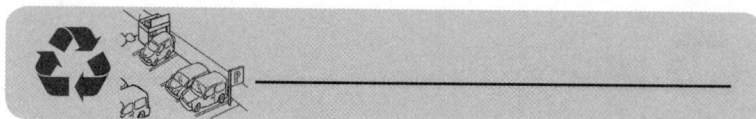

1 **Look and write.**

man   men   woman   women   child   children

1 one _____ man _____

2 two _____

3 _____

4 _____

5 _____

6 _____

2 **Read and listen. Match.** CD4 19

1 Who's that woman?

2 Who are those children?

3 Who's that man?

4 Who's that child?

5 Who are those men?

6 Who are those women?

POLICE STATION _____

1 Write and say.

ear – air. The b_ear_ with a p_____ climbs the st____s at the funf____.

2 Colour the 'ear' words blue and the 'air' words red. Say.

pear	hair	airport	stairs
chair	bear	wear	air

3 💬 **Talk Partners** Play *Snap* in pairs.

1, 2, 3 *hair!*

1, 2, 3 *pear!*

Snap!

1, 2, 3 *bear!*

1, 2, 3 *bear!*

Snap!

Play _Snap_: Pupils play with their Talk Partner. Pupils individually think of a word, count to three together, point to the picture and say the word. If the words are the same, they say *Snap*! If they are different, they continue playing the game.

1 **Listen and number. Write.**

CD4 23

play hide and seek   paint a cup   ~~see butterflies~~   play chess

see butterflies

💡 **Think about your culture**

What do you do in the summer holidays?

2  **Read and tick (✓). Draw, write and say.**

1 I visit a palace.

2 I play games in the park.

3 I go to an arts and crafts studio.

4 I see animals at the safari park.

5 I visit a museum.

I _____ .

After you read

Text type: **A diary**

1 Think about the diary. Read and write.

On Saturday, it was _____sunny_____ and _____.

I was at the _____. It was _____!

On Sunday, it was _____ and _____.

I was at the _____. It was _____!

2 Write your own diary and draw.

My diary

Yesterday was _____.

It was _____.

I was at _____

_____.

It was _____!

1 Find, circle and write.

W	O	M	A	N	D	S	O
A	C	H	I	L	D	T	R
M	E	N	J	Z	T	X	Y
M	M	F	M	M	A	N	P
W	O	M	E	N	F	R	S
C	H	I	L	D	R	E	N
A	T	O	S	M	N	N	E

1 _____child_____

2 _____

3 _____

4 _____

5 _____

6 _____

2 Read and write.

Who's that …?   Who are those …?

man   men   woman   women   ~~child~~   children

1 __Who's that child?_____ He's my brother.

2 _____ They're my aunts.

3 _____ They're my uncles.

4 _____ They're my cousins.

5 _____ He's my grandfather.

6 _____ She's my mother.

3 **My progress** Use your traffic light. Listen to the teacher and point.

Key for Activity 3: **1.** I can say and write the ten holiday place words. **2.** I can ask and answer about events in the past. **3.** I can talk about the summer holidays. **4.** I can read a diary. **5.** I can write my own diary.

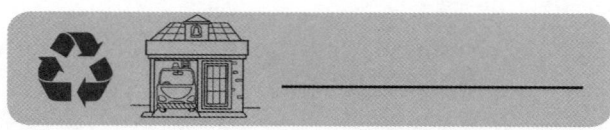

_____

Using a digital camera

1 Listen and tick (✓). 🖸 CD4 28

1

3

2

4

 **CHANNEL**

What do you take photos of?

2 **Think and write. Draw and say.**

I take photos of

1 _____.

2 _____.

3 _____.

4 _____.

_____ _____

Let's practise spelling!

Look	Copy	Cover and write
1 science museum	_____	_____
2 circus	_____	_____
3 castle	_____	_____
4 sports centre	_____	_____
5 funfair	_____	_____
6 safari park	_____	_____
7 aquarium	_____	_____
8 water park	_____	_____
9 theatre	_____	_____
10 chocolate factory	_____	_____

_____

TIME

18:23 1:30

Plan your project

1 **What time is it? Look and tick (✓).**

1  It's a quarter past ten. ✓
It's a quarter to ten. ◯

2  It's three o'clock. ◯
It's half past three. ◯

3  It's half past two. ◯
It's half past one. ◯

4  It's a quarter to eleven. ◯
It's a quarter to nine. ◯

5  It's six o'clock. ◯
It's seven o'clock. ◯

6  It's a quarter past seven. ◯
It's a quarter to seven. ◯

2 **What time is it? Write.**

1 It's eight o'clock .

2 _____
_____ .

3 _____
_____ .

4 _____
_____ .

5 _____
_____ .

1 Write about your day.

Remember

he she

1 I get up at

2 I get dressed at

3 I have breakfast at

4 I go to school at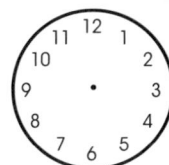

5 I play at

6 I go to bed at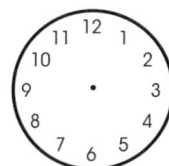

Think about your project

2 Read, think and colour the stars.

I listen to my friends.

I share my things.

I help my friends.

I make an effort.

I like my clock.

1   **Look and write.**

Play	Go
football	

2   **Follow and write.**

1

2

3

_____

_____

4

_____ hit _____

5

_____

6

_____

_____

1 Find, circle and write.

G	Y	O	G	H	U	R	T	R	F	J	Q
A	P	L	S	R	K	B	L	E	M	O	N
O	B	T	W	G	C	A	R	R	O	T	S
N	G	R	E	E	N	B	E	A	N	S	K
S	L	F	E	E	Q	R	D	C	H	S	L
S	P	O	T	A	T	O	E	S	M	D	E
R	M	S	S	T	O	M	A	T	O	E	S
L	D	B	R	E	A	D	E	F	S	W	Z

yoghurt

_____

_____

_____

_____

_____

2 Look and write.

1. 50

2. 20

3. 30

4. 40

5. 10

1 _fifty peaches_

2 _____

3 _____

4 _____

5 _____

3 Vocabulary practice

1 Look and write.

1 ___lion___

2 _____

3 _____

4 _____

5 _____

6 _____

7 _____

8 _____

9 _____

10 _____

2 Look and write.

1 A ___parrot___ has got big ___wings___.

2 A _____ has got a long _____.

3 A _____ has got big _____.

4 A _____ has got a long _____.

5 A _____ has got a big _____.

6 A _____ hasn't got a big _____.

1 **Find and circle. Write.**

FORESTGHILLRBRIDGEAROADSPATHSLAKE

1 _____forest_____   2 _____   3 _____

4 _____   5 _____   6 _____

Write the mystery word: __ __ __ __ __

2 **Read, match and write.**

1 He's running _____ the hill.

2 He's riding a bike _____ the road.

3 She's riding a horse _____down_____ the hill.

4 She's swimming _____ the bridge.

5 She's walking _____ the lake.

1   **Order the letters and write.**

1   e m s i l

_____smile_____

2   a k s t e

_____

3   a c e n d

_____

4   e k a t   a   h o o t p

_____

5   a w e v

_____

6   k r d i n

_____

7   y l p a

_____

2   **Follow and write.**

1 a _____clean_____ snowman

2 a _____ snowman

3 a _____ snowman

4 a _____ snowman

5 a _____ snowman

6 a _____ snowman

1 **Write and match.**

a

1 We _____plant seeds_____ in _____.

b

2 We _____ in _____.

c

3 We _____ in _____.

d

4 We _____ in _____.

2 **Look and write.**

1
My birthday is on the 1ˢᵗ

_____first_____ of April.

4
My birthday is on the 3ʳᵈ

_____ of March.

2
My birthday is on the 8ᵗʰ

_____ of May.

5
My birthday is on the 5ᵗʰ

_____ of August.

3
My birthday is on the 2ⁿᵈ

_____ of June.

1 Write the missing letters.

1

f l a t

2

h _ _ _ _ _

3

_ a r _ _ _ _

4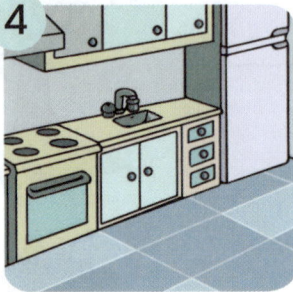

_ i _ _ _ e _

5

_ _ t _ _ _ o _

6

g _ _ _ _ _ _

2 Look and write.

1 There's a mouse in the _____ bedroom _____.

2 There's a camera in the _____.

3 There's a radio in the _____.

4 There's a car in the _____.

5 There's a watch in the _____.

6 There's a phone in the _____.

7 There's a clock in the _____.

8 There's a box in the

_____.

1 Read, write and match.

 a
 b
 c
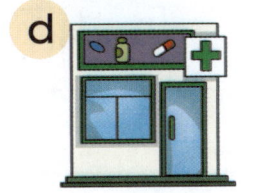 d
 e
 f
 g
 h

1 We buy bread at the _____ baker's _____.

2 We park the car at the _____.

3 We catch a train at the _____.

4 We post a letter at the _____.

5 We catch a bus at the _____.

6 We buy medicine at the _____.

7 We put money in at the _____.

8 We see dinosaurs at the _____.

2 Complete the conversation.

1 Where's the 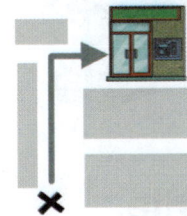 _____ bank _____?

Turn right.

2 Where's the 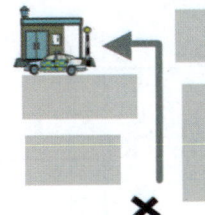 _____?

_____

_____

3 Where's the 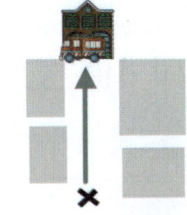 _____?

_____

_____

4 Where's the 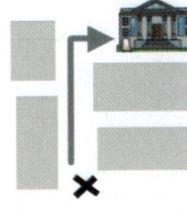 _____?

_____

_____

1 Write the holiday places. Where was Toby yesterday?

Yesterday, I was at the
_____ .

| | | | 1 | C | I | R | C | U | S | | |

2 Look and write.

1 The man is at the ___science museum___ .

2 The women are at the _____ .

3 The child is at the _____ .

4 The children are at the _____ .

5 The woman is at the _____ .

6 The men are at the _____ .

Reading and Writing

1 Read this. Choose a word from the box. Write the correct word next to numbers 1–6.

A ball

You can **1** __throw__ or **2** _____ me. I can be big or

3 _____. You can play **4** _____ with me. In football,

I am white and **5** _____. You can have a lot of fun with me at

the **6** _____. What am I? I'm a ball.

park small basketball tree

catch black big ~~throw~~

2 Look and read. Write *yes* or *no*.

1 There is a cat in the tree. __no__

2 The girls are playing football. _____

3 There is a big ball on the table. _____

4 The duck is swimming. _____

5 A boy is hitting a ball. _____

6 The tall girl has got long hair. _____

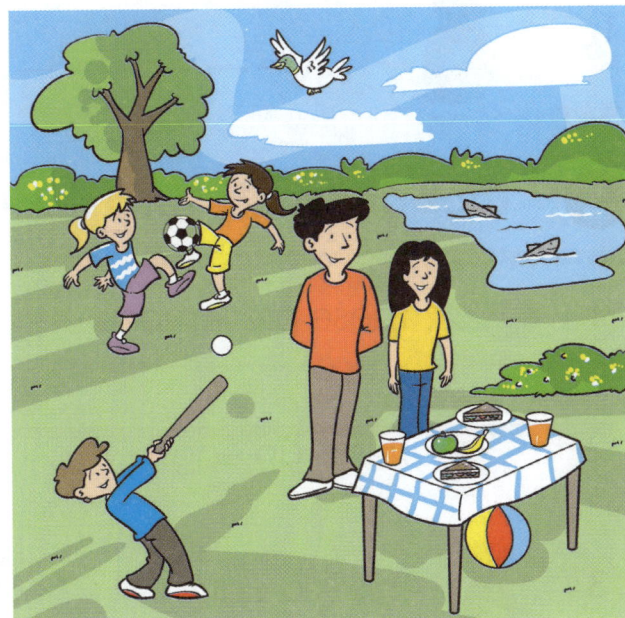

Reading and Writing

1 **Look at the picture. Look at the letters. Write the words.**

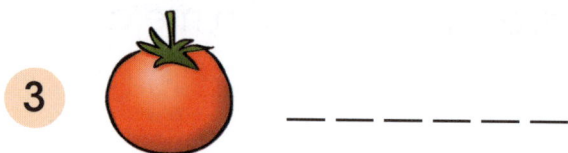

1 l _ _ _ _

m l n
e o

2 _ _ _ _ _

r a e
b d

3 _ _ _ _ _ _

a o o
t m t

4 _ _ _ _ _ _

a o r
c t r

5 _ _ _ _ _ _

t o o
a p t

6 _ _ _ _ _ _ _ _ _

a e l i
p n p e p

2 **Look and read. Put a tick (✓) or a cross (✗) in the box.**

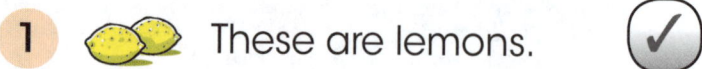

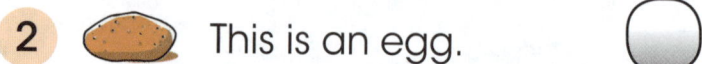

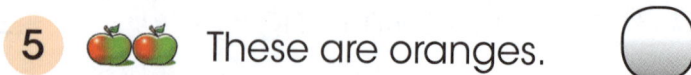

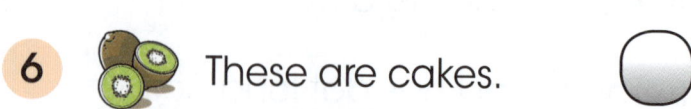

1 These are lemons. ✓   4 These are tomatoes. ◯

2 This is an egg. ◯   5 These are oranges. ◯

3 This is a carrot. ◯   6 These are cakes. ◯

Key learning outcome: practice for Reading and Writing Parts 3 and 1

Reading and Writing

1 Read and write the correct word. There is one example.

A penguin

I've got two **1** _____eyes_____ and two **2** _____. I live in the

zoo and I swim in the **3** _____. My favourite food is

4 _____. I'm **5** _____ and white. I haven't got

6 _____ because I'm a bird! What am I? I am a penguin.

black

water

face

hands

legs

carrots

fish

~~eyes~~

2 Look at the pictures. Look at the letters. Write the words.

1 c r o c o d i l e

c i d c r o e l o

2 _ _ _ _ _ _ _ _

a t h l p n e e

3 _ _ _ _ _ _ _

f f a e g r i

4 _ _ _ _ _ _

o m k n y e

5 _ _ _ _ _ _

r i z l a d

6 _ _ _ _ _

p i p o h

Reading and Writing

1 **Look and read. Write *yes* or *no*.**

1 A girl is swimming in the water. __yes__   2 A girl is playing basketball. _____

3 The frog is in front of the rabbit. _____   4 A boy is riding a bike. _____

5 There are three birds. _____   6 A boy is playing in the sand. _____

2 **Look at the picture and read the questions. Write one-word answers.**

1 Where's the helmet?

on the girl's _____ head _____

2 How many children are there?

_____

3 What's the boy doing?

He's _____

4 What's the girl riding?

a _____

5 Where's the fish?

in the _____

Key learning outcome: practice for Reading and Writing Parts 2 and 5

Reading and Writing

1 **Look and read. Write *yes* or *no*.**

1 A girl is eating a carrot. _____no_____   2 The cat is next to a lizard. _____

3 There are three birds in a tree. _____   4 The tall girl has got an apple. _____

5 Two boys are waving. _____   6 The small girl is smiling. _____

2 **Look at the picture and read the questions. Write one-word answers.**

1 What are the boys doing?

taking a _____photo_____

2 What's the boy eating?

a _____

3 Who's swimming?

a _____

4 What are the girls doing?

_____

5 How many girls are there?

_____

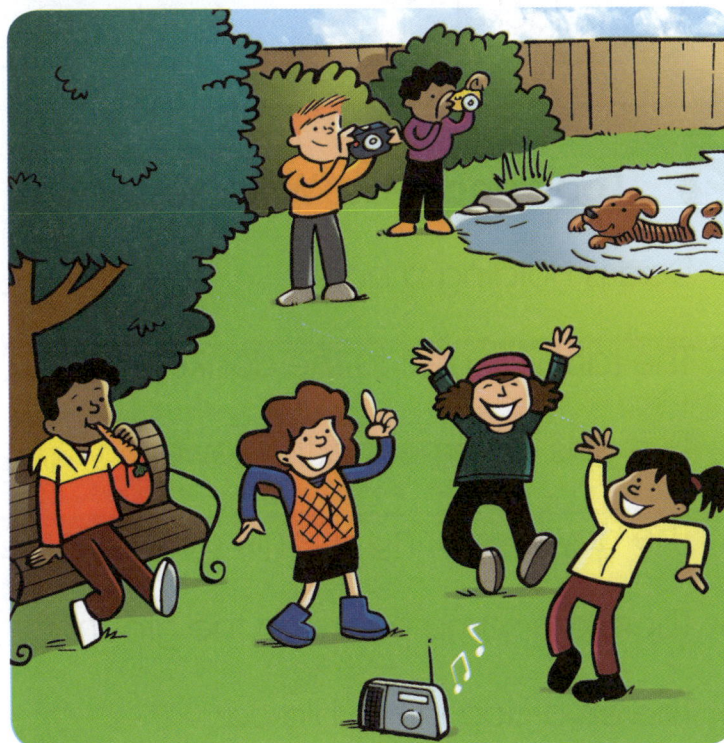

Key learning outcome: practice for Reading and Writing Parts 2 and 5

Reading and Writing

1 Read and write the correct word. There is one example.

Autumn

I'm one of the **1** ___four___ seasons. Leaves change **2** _____

and fall down from the **3** _____. It starts to get

4 _____. You wear a **5** _____ and eat

6 _____. What am I? I am autumn.

four

colour

trees

grass

jacket

cold

hot

chestnuts

2 Look and read. Write *yes* or *no*.

1 Dad is holding a ball. ___yes___

2 The rabbit is next to the donkey. _____

3 Two girls are smelling the flowers. _____

4 The boy is wearing a T-shirt and shorts. _____

5 There are some pears on the ground. _____

6 There's a dog in the big car. _____

Key learning outcome: practice for Writing Parts 4 and 2

Reading and Writing

1 Look at the picture and read the questions. Write one-word answers.

1 Where are the children?   in the _____ *living* _____ room

2 What's the girl doing?   _____ TV

3 What's the boy reading?   a _____

4 Where's the clock?   on the _____

5 How many flowers are there?   _____

2 Look at the pictures. Look at the letters. Write the words.

1 _k i t c h e n_
t c e h i n k

2 _ _ _ _ _ _ _   _ _ _ _
g l v i i n   r m o o

3 _ _ _ _ _ _ _
d r m o b o e

4 _ _ _ _ _ _ _   _ _ _ _
i i n n d g   o r o m

5 _ _ _ _ _ _ _ _
b t o h a o m r

6 _ _ _ _ _ _
n d r g a e

Reading and Writing

1 **Look and read. Write yes or no.**

1 There's a bank next to the chemist's.   _yes_

2 There are three trees in the park.   _____

3 There's a dog running in front of the police station.   _____

4 There's a post office between the fire station and the train station.   _____

5 There aren't any museums.   _____

2 **Look at the pictures. Look at the letters. Write the words.**

1 _b a n k_
k a b n

2 _ _ _ _
r k p a

3 _ _ _
o z o

4 _ _ _ _ _ _
h o l c s o

5 _ _ _ _ _ _
u m m u e s

6 _ _ _ _ _ _ _
a r c k a p r

Key learning outcome: practice for Reading and Writing Parts 2 and 3

Reading and Writing

1 Look at the picture and read the questions. Write one-word answers.

1 How many cars are there? _____ *three* _____

2 What's the boy doing? playing with a _____

3 What's the girl doing? drinking _____

4 Where's the woman? next to the _____

5 What's the dog doing? _____

6 How many flowers are there? _____

2 Look and read. Put a tick (✓) or a cross (✗) in the box.

1 This is a man. ✓

2 These are women. ◯

3 This is a castle. ◯

4 This is a school. ◯

5 This is a sports centre. ◯

6 These are children. ◯

Macmillan Education
4 Crinan Street
London N1 9XW
A division of Macmillan Publishers Limited

Companies and representatives throughout the world

Activity Book 978-1-380-01377-4

This edition published 2018
First edition entitled *High Five! English* published 2014 by Macmillan
Publishers Limited

Original series concept design by Tom Cole
Designed by Anthony Godber
Page makeup by emc design ltd
Illustrated by Kathy Baxendale, Leo Broadley, Sam Church, Nigel
Dobbyn, Joelle Dreidemy, Clive Goodyer, Andy Keylock, Andy Painter,
Dusan Pavlic, Ángeles Peinador, Andy Robb, Mark Ruffle, Jorge
Santillán, Eric Smith, Simon Smith, Sholto Walker and Matt Ward.
Cover design by Bigtop Design Limited
Cover photographs by **Getty Images**/iStockphoto/Thinkstock Images/
katsto80; Tom Dick and Debbie Productions
Cover illustration by Ángeles Peinador
Songs produced and arranged by Tom Dick and Debbie Productions
Recordings produced and arranged by Footsteps and Tom Dick and
Debbie Productions
Picture research by Sally Cole and Fernanda Rocha/Ikonia LLC

Authors' acknowledgements
The authors would like to thank everyone at Macmillan who has given
help and advice throughout this project. Special thanks from Jo to
Carlos, Daniel and Alex for their patience and support during this
process. Special thanks from Donna to José, Elisa, Teresa and Marina
for their encouragement and enthusiasm.

Acknowledgments
The publishers would like to thank the following teachers for their
contribution to the project:
Amanda Morrison Prince, Colegio El Parque, La Navata, Madrid;
Amaya Carrera García, Colegio Santa Teresa de Jesús, Valladolid;
Ana Fernández Sáez, CEIP La Encina, Las Rozas, Madrid; Aránzazu
Sánchez Rodríguez, CEIP Rosa Luxemburgo, Madrid; Beatriz García
Vaquero, CEIP Mariano José de Larra, Madrid; Carme Tena, Col·legi
Sagrada Familia, Tortosa, Tarragona; Cristina Nieto Ruíz de Gaona,
CEIP Margarita Salas, Arroyo de la Encomienda, Valladolid; Estíbaliz
Medina Martín, CEIP Virgen de Navalazarza, San Agustín de Guadalix,
Madrid; Iratxe Zabaleta Zendagorta, Ikastola San Fidel, Guernica,
Vizcaya; Lucía Soria García, CEIP Alberto Alcocer, Madrid; M.ª
Carmen Lago Muñoz, CEIP Federico García Lorca, Colmenar Viejo,
Madrid; Marta Moreno Arroyo, CEIP Vicente Aleixandre, Móstoles,
Madrid; Susana Espinel Beneitez, Colegio Grazalema, El Puerto de
Santa María, Cádiz; Susana García Pizarro, Ateneu Instructiu, Sant
Joan Despi, Barcelona; Virgina Escalona Monreal, CEIP La Encina,
Las Rozas, Madrid; Mónica Pérez Is, CEIP Reina Victoria, Madrid;
Rocío Gutierrez, CEIP Lepanto, Madrid; Laura Zarzuelo, Colegio
Virgen de la Almudena, Collado Villalba, Madrid; Eugenio Domínguez,
Colegio Virgen de la Almudena, Collado Villalba, Madrid; Silvia Díez
de Rivera, Colegio Orvalle, Las Rozas, Madrid; Maite Crespo, Colegio
Jesús Nazareno, Madrid; Silvia Valderrama, CEIP Benito Pérez
Galdós, Arganda del Rey, Madrid; Cristina Baeza, CEIP Rosa Chacel,
Collado Villalba, Madrid; Leyre Alcalde, CEIP Cortes de Cádiz, Madrid;
María Andrés, Colegio Matter Inmaculata, Madrid.

The authors and publishers would like to thank the following for
permission to reproduce their photographs:
Alamy Stock Photo/q77photo p85(top banner); **Getty Images**/
Dorling Kindersley/Tim Ridley 75(top banner), Getty Images/E+/
vpopovic pp111-119(top banner), Getty Images/iStock/Vjom p63(top
banner), Getty Images/Jeffoto p95(top banner), Getty Images/PJB/
Photographer's Choice p31(top banner), Getty Images/Jaskunwar
Singh/EyeEm p11(top banner); **Macmillan Publishers Ltd.**/Lisa Payne
pp11(c), 21, 31(c), 43(c), 53(c), 63(c), 75(c), 85(c), 95(c); **Plainpicture**/
Johner/Roine Magnusson p43(top banner); **Shutterstock**/ber1a
p53(top banner), Shutterstock/OnlyFOOD p22.

Commissioned photography by Lisa Payne (pp11, 21, 22, 31, 36, 43,
53, 63, 68, 75, 85, 95, 100) and Tom Dick and Debbie Productions
(pp14, 24, 34, 46, 56, 66, 78, 88, 98).

Printed and bound in Spain

2023   2022   2021   2020
16   15   14   13   12   11   10